Letters

FROM A

Father

Allen Carter

Additional Praise for Letters from a Father

- There is an overflow of wisdom in ***Letters From A Father***. From learning how to love from a dog to spending time with our creator, this book is sure to make you a better father to all the children you have been called to lead.

  Blake Wright, Three of Seven Project

- Please read this book and perhaps start writing to the kids in your life. ***Letters from a Father*** is priceless.

  Bob Muzikowski, Founder and President,
  Chicago Hope Academy

ISBN 978-1-64300-793-9 (Paperback)
ISBN 978-1-64300-794-6 (Digital)

Covenant Books, Inc.
11661 Hwy 707
Murrells Inlet, SC 29576
www.covenantbooks.com

Contents

Acknowledgements

More than anything, I am grateful to God who has blessed me with such a beautiful and loving family. My wife, Mary, and my three children; Claire, Wells and Emma, are the light of my life, my joy and my reason for being. Thank you, dear family, for your support of me as a new author and for your willingness to open our lives for all to see.

Thanks also to my parents—this book was their idea. Years ago, a few of the first letters to Claire were shared with them and in tears they asked me to share them with the world. The decision to do so was not an easy one. These letters were simply the private musings of one father to his children. I was not at all sure that I wanted anyone else's eyes on them (or on us as a family). Now that we are here, it is my hope that they are helpful and that they may strengthen the bonds of the families they touch.

Thank you also to Bob Muzikowski who graciously penned the Foreword. Bob has single handedly changed the outcome for thousands of kids' lives through his work in the Chicago Little Leagues and at The Chicago Hope Academy. He received worldwide recognition when they made the movie, *Hardball*, about him in 2001 featuring Keanu Reeves. Although if you ask him, Hollywood got the story wrong.

I am really thankful to the whole team at Covenant Books, especially Michelle Holmes and Ladonna Giessmann. Working with a new author must be excruciating but they were both kind and steady guides.

To my mentors and friends; my awesome team at work, my accountability partner, Rob Cressy, and the friends who have given me advice and counsel as it relates to this project—especially to Brian

Portnoy. A shout out also to the influencers who have helped form and guide me—Ed Mylett, Darren Hardy and Jessie Itzler. It's people like these who remind all of us that nothing is impossible.

Now to Him who is able to do immeasurably more
than all that we ask or imagine, according to His power that
is at work within us.

Ephesians 3:20

Foreword

It was a beautiful afternoon in Chicago. I was walking along LaSalle Street headed back to my office from a business meeting. It is one of Chicago's busiest streets.

But I'm from New York and Chicago has no packed pedestrian streets. I was headed north when a voice called out, "Coach Bob!"

It was Melvyn Hayes.

I coached Melvyn in the Near West Little League when it was the largest inner city baseball league in America with sixty-four teams. It had come a long way. I started it years before on a trash filled lot with a few neighborhood kids who were standing on the corner. The league is still going strong with thirty teams. We moved it to the west side of Chicago when Cabrini Green was demolished and they took our field away at Division and Sedgwick streets.

Anyway, Melvyn was the catcher for the Northwestern Mutual Orioles. I had been a catcher from age nine through high school. How did Melvyn and I become catchers? It's simple. The other kids wouldn't do it in July and August because it got really hot wearing the catcher's equipment. And…if diagnosed…we were both control freaks by age ten.

We embraced there on LaSalle Street. Hugged real hard. It had been twenty years. So Melvyn's now about thirty-two. He was working downtown, well dressed, eloquent, making a living and providing for his family. His "thank yous for coaching me" got us both a bit emotional. He promised to come out and see a Northwestern Little League game the following Saturday.

As Melvyn and I were saying our goodbyes I saw a face over his shoulder. A businessman seemed to stop and watch Melvyn and me interact. Our eyes connected.

"Something about him was familiar. I could swear I'd seen his face before."—Harry Chapin.

Initially I thought he was a former league baseball coach. Then I thought maybe he was an old Columbia University classmate. But then again, this guy looked way too good to be my age (it turns out we are ten years apart). He was neither of those. For some reason, we shook hands, exchanged a few words and went on our way. A few days later he called me.

His name is Allen Carter, a highly successful UBS Wealth Management Advisor. I "coincidentally" had an office in the UBS Tower on Madison and Wacker. We chatted a bit and agreed to get together for coffee.

I didn't think Allen would reach back out to get it scheduled but he did.

There are no coincidences. We had coffee and Allen was a guy I just liked right out of the gate. We quickly became friends at a very deep level.

To give you some background on my story:

It was mid April, 1996. Although it might still snow in Chicago, my first Little League Baseball practice was about to start.

My wife, friends and I started the Near North Little League in Cabrini Green in 1991. The league received a ton of unsolicited publicity. When we moved to the west side, we started the Near West Little League, leaving the Near North program in very good hands. By the late 90's the League had grown to over sixty teams, mostly boys but also with twelve girls' softball teams.

Almost all of our players came from the projects; the Henry Horner Homes (The Hornets), Rockwell Gardens, The Abla Homes (The Village), or St. Stephens (The Saints). All of us were volunteers and we all knew the League had little to do with baseball. It was about relationships, mentoring, assisting players and their families and the learning and stability that comes from simply showing up on time, every time for sixteen games, thirty-two practices and one road trip weekend to Little League tournaments from Dubuque, Iowa to a full week in Cooperstown, New York.

Unlike most Little Leagues in America that run April through June to allow for July and August family vacations, we played Memorial Day to Labor Day. Our league families were from almost all single parent or no parent families. They were not going to The Hamptons, or to Northern Michigan. The League itself and the creative picnics around the games were their vacations.

Most players signed up and were placed on teams out of a pool. But in the early years, I got my teams by taking a full equipment bag and buckets of baseballs over to Touhy Herbert Field, seven blocks from my house. If I got there by 3:00 PM - I'd have fifteen boys by 6:00 PM.

After that first practice, my new players were gassed from competitive sprints around the bases and bear hug contests held so the chubby kids could win. We also open and close every practice and game with prayer. I'm still waiting for the ACLU to stop the prayers as we are in a public park. But if they come, they won't have a car to drive home in. When there is often the background noise of gunfire (no exaggeration) during practice - you pray before, after and during everything.

Two of my new ten year olds, Keshon and Corey were left-handed throwers. They did not know that until this first practice. I called my wife who was home with our growing brood to come pick me up and bring two right-handed gloves from our garage (the league storage bin). When Tina got out of our station wagon Keshon asked me, "Who's that lady, Coach?"

I responded—"That's my wife."

Corey and Keshon simultaneously asked, "She be livin' wit you?"

They were ten years old and did not know what "wife" meant. Obviously, they did not know what "husband' meant either. And that my friends is one of the reasons that **Letters From a Father** is a must read for all Dads whether they live with their children or not.

In my twenty-eight years of coaching and parenting boys and girls, I rarely meet fathers. When I do, we become very close. Willie Naugles and Charlie Williams were good friends and Alcoholics Anonymous buddies until they died. Most of the boys I coached for three or four years never had a father come to a game despite my great efforts to make that happen. Fatherhood IS the number one issue here. Forget all the politically correct bull**** coming from people who have never personally had fatherless boys become part of their family.

At one point we had eleven young people living with us - our seven biological children and four fatherless African American young men. I'm still close to everybody and even my own kids talk to me every week (that was my warped sense of humor).

A father is the best protector, mentor and leader a kid can have. Not having one, by the father's choice - not because he died, makes having emotional and financial well being very, very tough.

For thirty years, I've written to my kids in a big hard-bound diary. I forget where I got the idea. It's full of what they were doing at various ages - stuff and historical events from different chapters in their lives. It's been great for me and they will laugh out loud when their Mom and I present it to them at their weddings or whenever the moment is right.

Your letters don't have to be brilliant. But I'm begging you to read this book and start writing to your kids.

Letters from a father are....priceless.

Bob Muzikowski
Founder and President, Chicago Hope Academy
Founder, Near North and Near West Little Leagues

Introduction

I love my kids just as most fathers do. We want the best for them. We want them to be happy, to flourish, to live lives of abundance, joy, and fulfillment. We want them to achieve their dreams and become everything that they were created to be.

We want them to be safe also. We crave protection for them—not just in the physical sense but also insulation from the emotional and psychological scratches that come in the course of adolescence. We hurt when they hurt, cry when they cry and feel pain when things go against them.

There is regret too for all of us. Sometimes searing regret.

There are many times when we were not there and should have been. We put other things first— work, selfish pleasures, whatever it was at the time that seemed more important. Oh—my heart aches for those times, and my eyes well with tears when I look back. Not just for the events I missed due to some meeting somewhere but rather the small things. The precious touch of my son or daughter as they lay in my arms with a book. The look in their young eyes of love and admiration for a father who they think is the greatest—simply because I have devoted some time to them.

As fathers, we justify missing time with our kids by blaming work obligations or a need for "balance" in our lives. We say to ourselves that the best way to provide for our family is by giving them financial security. Is it? What does the concept of financial security mean anyway? My experience tells me that there is a massive gap between putting food on the table and the way that each father defines financial security. For me, the term meant significant monetary wealth. Coming from that was an endless striving to keep up with neighbors and friends in one of America's most affluent suburbs. The trek was an exhausting one, and in all honesty, an endless one.

As found by most of those who pursue wealth as a goal, I discovered that no amount of it produces satisfaction or peace. There is no reaching the mountaintop and no hitting a certain number that causes you to stand down or relax. There is never enough.

The outcome of this type of pursuit (or any other) is a massive time suck that robs a family of their father's attention, presence, and engagement. The results can be terrible of course. Statistics clearly show how kids can get challenged quickly when there is no father figure engaged in their lives. Incarceration and crime are worst-case scenarios but what about the more common outcomes? Here I am referring to kids who grow up directionless. Lives lived with quiet frustration. Dreams left unfulfilled or unpursued. People dying with the music still inside of them.

We as fathers can change all of that. The power we have is almost immeasurable. Through our love, focus, encouragement, and guidance, we can impart to our children gifts beyond description. We can instill in their lives beliefs and values that will allow them to be who they want to be and become who they want to become.

As I realized this in my own life, I began to write a monthly letter to my children during their teenage years. For me, it was just a way to supplement our day-to-day interaction. A way to highlight experiences or call attention to lessons we all were being taught in our journey together.

In this book, there are more than sixty letters covering an array of topics that will give you an unintentional glimpse of my family. Without a doubt, you will find that our struggles, observations, and landmarks are very similar to yours. It turns out that we all face the same challenges, and it is this connection that makes things relevant. The role of God and faith-based values are highlighted throughout the letters, and stories from the Bible are used frequently. It is not my intent to foist religion upon people though the amount of wisdom and promise in the scriptures flat out cannot be ignored or glossed over.

So in summation, what choices will you make for those children in your life? Will you give them these gifts? Will you put them before your own interests? If you do, you will impart the richest of blessings to them and interestingly enough uncover happiness and peace for yourself.

The First Letter

Love

Dear Claire and Wells,

You may remember the time you took when you were very young before climbing a new tree. It was difficult for you to look up at the challenge especially when that first limb was a good distance from the ground. The first few moves were the hardest. I remember you guys heaving onto trees repeatedly trying to get started, the first branch just out of reach. In a way, it is my turn now to have these feelings as I commit to writing to my two teenagers regularly over the coming year. I know that we talk, cry, and laugh together often, and these letters to you will never replace our conversations (as trying as some of them must be). Rather, I am hopeful that the letters will quietly speak to you when you are willing to listen to my heart and thoughts rather than my voice.

I love you both so much that it defies the description of words. It is a deep and resonant love— one of fatherhood and nature, God-given, and as timeless as the heavens. It can withstand anything and it is impossible to break. So it makes sense to start with some thoughts about love.

The emotion of love is the single most powerful force on the planet. I can add little to the volumes written on the subject, but I can describe to you what it means to me.

Love for me is simply placing another person's needs and wants above my own. The closer I am to someone, the stronger my urge to do such a thing. When it comes to you and our family, there is no good thing that I would not do for you—no need of my own that I would put ahead of yours. Stay with me here, I will admit that my own selfish desires can knock down my noble intentions. I recall when my own want for some quiet time or the pursuit of a hobby or any number of other distractions have temporarily sidetracked me from putting your desires first. I hope that when this happens, you will forgive me. I also hope that when this happens, it impacts only little things. When it comes to your health, safety, future, happiness, and success though, there is no way that I wouldn't always put you guys first. Every time. No questions. I hope that you know this, and I hope that you recognize my love for you through the trying times or when decisions I make seem unreasonable or senseless in the heat of my role as your father.

Here's the big thing about love. Humans are broken and flawed. We exist to please ourselves and are constantly trying to fill voids in our lives with things, pursuits, and people that we think will make us happy. You may be finding out already in your lives that none of that works. Advertising, television, and every other input always suggest that if you would purchase something or look like someone, you will be successful and happy. That's a lie. The only way to achieve fulfillment and joy in this life is by living a life full of love. A life where you place your own interests and desires behind those of others. In a sense, the act of loving someone provides a much greater gift for the giver than for the one who receives.

The final piece is simply this: you can't do it alone. God is ultimately the author of love, and it is only through Him that we can truly be filled with love and fulfilled as people. So love freely, put one another's needs ahead of your own, and seek daily to know the author of love even if you doubt His presence at times.

With much love,
Dad

The Second Letter

Science and Faith

Dear Claire and Wells,

Science is not exact despite what scientists want you to believe. To be sure, science and the pursuit of knowledge through its study are essential. Through science, humanity has made huge gains in all aspects of our existence. However, it is changeable, fraught with flaws, errors, and theories that change incredibly often.

Here is a simple example: up until the fourth century BC, the earth was proven by science to be flat. The spherical shape of the earth was then proposed by Aristotle. For the next two thousand years, science supposed that the earth was the center of the universe (geocentricism). It wasn't until the sixteenth century that the sun was definitively proven to be the center of the universe (heliocentricism). Believe it or not, guys, it was less than one hundred years ago that we discovered that the universe was a tad bigger than our little solar system. The universe might consist of billions of solar systems like ours. *Science* has no real clue on it yet.

You can see that the passage of time and technological advancements make short work of scientific "proofs." It will be incredibly interesting to see what other theorems are torn down in the course of our lifetimes. It is really important to view science as a wonderful servant but recognize that it can be a terrible master. Just think about Hitler and Germany of only about seventy years ago, the Nazi devotion to science and the pursuit of Aryan genetic superiority led to horrific and unspeakable things. Here's my point: science by itself cannot provide all the answers. It cannot be relied upon. It's a car with only one wheel. There's something more.

That something more is called faith.

You can go almost anywhere for a definition of the word *faith*, but I think the best one resides in the Bible in Hebrews 11:1: "Now faith is the assurance of things hoped for, the belief of things not seen." For me, it comes down to an unwavering and unshakable belief in things that neither science nor I can touch, see, or explain. It's a powerful force in me and in others who espouse it. If you read further in Hebrews 11, you'll see vivid examples about how individuals with deep faith changed the course of history.

It comes down to this. Life without faith is a very empty and sometimes dangerous thing. Individuals who rely on themselves or science for answers or direction are invariably disheartened and disappointed. The "leap" of faith is much like the famed "trust fall" into the arms of your old dad. After you committed and landed in my arms, there is a feeling of warmth, love, and belief. Live a life of deep faith!

Love you!
Dad

The Third Letter

Seeing Clearly

Dear Claire and Wells,

You know by now that the Bible fascinates me. Some view it as just another book on the shelf, others as a collection of random and sometimes conflicting stories. I know better. Every time I open that book, I find it fresh and new. Its pages never fail to yield insight and wisdom no matter how many times they have been read.

A few weeks ago, you'll remember that I took a trip to Wilmington, Delaware, to visit my mother and father. They are older now—with my father's cancer clouding their future. As we walked around their house together, we lingered over one of my father's recent paintings. It was a masterful copy of a famous work produced by the great Caravaggio entitled *Supper at Emmaus*. The piece was one of my father's finest and beautifully depicted Jesus breaking bread with two of his disciples. The story goes like this…

Jesus was killed and buried, his disciples scattered and terrified. Three days later, on the most important day in all of history, he rose from the dead and like nothing ever happened began visiting his followers. In pre-technology days, word traveled very slowly, and the region began to be set aflame by rumors and accounts of the dead Christ walking and appearing everywhere. You could only imagine the uproar. So two of Jesus' disciples were walking to Emmaus from Jerusalem, a seven-mile distance and were of course talking about the rumors of a risen Christ. A man joined them in their walk and in their conversation, and after the day's journey, he sat with them for dinner, gave thanks for the bread, broke it, and passed it to them.

Their eyes were opened, and they recognized Jesus. It was this particular moment in time that my father's painting captured and it was absolutely electrifying. You could see clearly the shock and tension of the revelation in the faces and hands of the disciples. One disciple gripped the table so firmly that you think it just might break. Jesus then disappeared from sight, and they immediately get up and trek back to Jerusalem (at great risk to themselves given the crime levels at night on the highways back then) to share the news with fellow followers.

Here's the thing: even though these two disciples had worked and lived with Jesus for years, they did not recognize him. Even more amazingly, Mary Magdalene who was as close to Jesus as anyone did not know who he was on the morning of his resurrection. How is this possible?

Human beings tend to wander through life focused on very few things. On the top of that very short list, you will find that the average person is focused predominantly on themselves. What a waste! Think of the beauty around us, the love that we can experience, and the opportunities we have to give. Now back to the story above, these disciples on the road to Emmaus and Mary Magdalene could not even recognize that the God of the universe was right there next to them. They were blinded by fear, the noise in their own lives, their own self-absorption, and their own flawed sense about what was important.

The lesson for all of us is fairly straightforward. God exists in every person that crosses your path. We are called to pay attention and recognize him in other people. When we seek, God promises that we will find. Maybe if the disciples and Mary Magdalene had this understanding, they would have instantly recognized the Lord.

We need to seek opportunities to serve and love. When we do this, our eyes and our souls are opened up; we can see clearly God in others and experience a life that is truly full.

Love you both so much!
Dad

The Fourth Letter

Self-Discipline

Dear Claire and Wells,

It will come as no surprise to you that the content of this particular letter will be focused on one of the greatest of all human strengths. You have heard me talk about it all your lives and are probably surprised that it took me so long to write to you on it. The strength I refer to is of course self-discipline.

I want to be clear at the outset that when I say this strength is a human one, you also understand that it is God-given. Additionally, without a reliance on God's constant grace, this strength in our lives becomes tenuous and even impossible to maintain. Humans at our best are pretty fragile creatures subject to selfish whims and desires that constantly throw us off course. Self-discipline, even in the strongest of men, cannot be a certain thing without the power of God bolstering it. Your mother has rightly said that given the right circumstances and the wrong timing, even the best of us are capable of the most egregious things. She is correct (as usual) and her point is important. We must focus on relying always on our Lord's grace and mercy to keep us from destructive paths and wrong choices. That being said, self-discipline is an incredible power in your life and when encouraged, practiced, developed, and honed can shape your life like nothing else. Bottom line—you can do anything you set your mind upon.

At its core, self-discipline is nothing more than a desire hierarchy. In other words, if faced with two attractive alternatives, self-discipline would cause you to select the alternative that is more important and more beneficial to you. Let's say that you want to lose weight, but you also want to indulge in a delicious (and very fattening) desert. Self-discipline would allow you to make the correct choice and forego the desert. It sounds simple but does not account for the fact that foregoing a short-term pleasure can be a very difficult thing. So here you have it: correct choices are often the most difficult ones and require solid discipline to make consistently.

In fact, Claire and Wells, you will probably find that almost without exception in your life, the correct choice in every scenario will be the more difficult one. Invariably choosing the path of most resistance will yield by far the greatest benefit. The examples are endless: going to the gym or working out when you do not feel like it, terminating unhealthy relationships, studying an extra hour for a test, withstanding peer pressure, doing the right thing when no one is looking, not cutting corners. Every one of these choices requires self–discipline, and every one of these choices will make you better, stronger, happier, and more fulfilled. Keep this as a key thought: whenever you are faced with a choice or a decision, no matter how big or small, take the path of most resistance.

Honing discipline in yourself does not come easily. It is a muscle that must be exercised and a trait that must be practiced. Remember first that it is God-given and grace directed, so the pursuit of self-discipline in your life should always include prayer and a deep conversation with God asking for his strength as you seek daily to choose the paths of most resistance. Here's another thought best conveyed by an anonymous and well-worn riddle:

> I am your constant companion. I am your greatest helper or your heaviest burden. I will push you onward or drag you down to failure. I am completely at your command. Half the things you do, you might as well just turn over to me, and I will be able to do them quickly and cor-

rectly. I am easily managed; you must merely be firm with me. Show me exactly how you want something done, and after a few lessons, I will do it automatically. I am the servant of all great men. And alas, of all failures as well. Those who are great, I have made great. Those who are failures, I have made failures. I am not a machine, though I work with all the precision of a machine. Plus, the intelligence of a man. You may run me for profit, or run me for ruin; it makes no difference to me. Take me, train me, be firm with me, and I will put the world at your feet. Be easy with me, and I will destroy you.

The question for the riddle is: Who am I? The answer? A Habit.

Claire and Wells, use your self-discipline to form good habits. As you do so, you will find that making positive choices and choosing paths of most resistance gets routine and in some cases, fairly easy. I am hesitant to end here. I am afraid that I have not conveyed adequately the importance of my thoughts around self-discipline in your lives. I do not want to lecture; I just want you to understand how important this concept is.

I love you both so much,
Dad

The Fifth Letter

Anxiety

Dear Claire and Wells,

There is a life stealer out there. Something that can drain you and rob your strength, energy, enthusiasm, and joy. It is the only emotion that in my view is wholly unproductive. It has no redeeming qualities. It serves no purpose other than to subvert our happiness. It is something that I have struggled with for much of my life. It is anxiety.

I often think about the origin of worry. It has been part of the human condition for as far back as history has been recorded. It probably originated as a by-product of the fear reflex. Remember that in its most basic form, the emotion of fear is a very healthy warning system hardwired into us. Fear alerts us of danger. Anxiety and worry do no such thing.

"Don't worry. Be happy" is an oft used phrase and the main tagline of the Disney movie classic, *The Lion King*. It sounds so simple. As easy as flipping a light switch. You have found already I am sure that actually ceasing to worry or harbor anxiety is a far more difficult feat. The mastery of anxiety is a hard road and one on which I am just learning to travel. Following are a few thoughts to help you on your road:

Experience

This is a tough one because by definition, it indicates that there is no quick solution. Experience applies to the mastery of anxiety

28

because you will realize as you get older that all things work out for the best.

This is a very hard concept to grasp especially when you are going through difficult times or are the victim of a bad circumstance. Nevertheless, it is quite true. Events often do not unfold the way you expect or desire, but over the long term, you will always realize when your attitude is correct, the results produced are character forming and positive. Forgive me for throwing this in but once again the Bible has a neat reference on this. Paul writes in Romans 8:28, "And we know that God causes all things to work together for good to those who love God, to those who are called according to his purpose." My point here is that anxiety or worry about how something will or will not turn out is irrelevant. It will work out for the best no matter what.

Preparation

There are two sets of variables in any given scenario, the set that we can control and the set that we cannot. For the former, through adequate preparation, we can almost guarantee how a situation will play out. It's the other set that poses a problem and the one that easily throws us into an anxiety state. Here's the question: Why worry about something over which you have no control? Easy answer. If you find that you cannot change something, leave it, and don't worry about it. Concentrate on the things that you can control.

Submission

The word *submission* is not a popular one in our society. It wrongfully connotes weakness. Nothing could be farther from the truth. It takes a very strong person to release concerns, anxieties, and frustrations. The interesting thing is this: when we release these things to God through prayer, we receive amazing peace. Here are more writings from St. Paul, this time from Philippians. A footnote on this by the way. When Paul was writing to the Philippians, he was being held in a dungeon in Rome. He was in chains and likely being starved and tortured. When you read Philippians, the first thing that you come away with is his joy and enthusiasm. Interesting, yes? At any rate, listen to these words from Philippians 4:6–7, "Be anxious for nothing, but in everything by prayer and supplication with thanksgiving let your requests be made known to God. And the peace of God, which surpasses all comprehension, shall guard your hearts and minds in Christ Jesus." Paul's meaning is clear, when we are able to open our hands and hearts, release our worries and anxieties through prayer and meditation, our joy and peace are hugely enhanced.

Worry and anxiety are emotions of which I want you so badly to be free. I hope that this letter has given you a few tools to work with. Be patient but consistent. Don't let your joy be stolen.

I love you both so much!
Dad

The Sixth Letter

Lucy

Dear Claire and Wells,

Our dog, Lucy, is a funny little creature. It's an amazing thing that God has imbued animals with such distinct personalities, emotions, and qualities. Lucy only weighs about fifteen pounds or so but has a personality that is far more substantial. There is no disputing that she can be incredibly frustrating at times with her bad habits and annoying tendencies, but overall she is a sweet and loving thing with a huge desire to win our love and approval. She was near me (as usual) the other day, and I took some time to reflect on what we might learn from her.

Lucy is loyal. She loves every one of us but for some reason has chosen to form a special bond with me. She will follow me everywhere if I allow it regardless of my mood, destination, purpose, or intent. In the morning after my shower, I will let her out, feed her, and then she will join me during my prayer and quiet time, follow me upstairs as I change for work, and down to the kitchen again before I depart. Her exuberance upon my reappearance in the evening is always something to see and never wavers. What an amazing quality is her loyalty! We can learn much from it and strive in our own lives to have the same faithfulness to each other. I pray that I would be as intensely committed to you both and to all those whom I love. No matter what.

Lucy is contrite. You both are very familiar with her shortcomings and bad habits. Despite our efforts, she retains a few quirks that are truly irritating. She is flawed as we all are. Here's the interesting thing though—when caught in the act or brought back to the scene of the issue, she immediately demonstrates her remorse, contrition, and guilt in a forthright and pitiable fashion. There is no pride, no denial, no blame. Just a sorrowful and contrite heart. Another great lesson for us. We all fall far short of what we could be.

We make constant mistakes, we hurt people that we love, and we have bad habits that are hard to break. I pray that when these things happen in my life, I will be quick to accept responsibility, demonstrate a sorrowful and contrite heart, and beg for your forgiveness with no pride or blame.

Lucy is full of life. We laugh at her passions and fancies. The way she tears across the yard in a pointless and never ending pursuit of the bikers on Sheridan Road is perplexing and silly. Her desire to chase every squirrel in the neighborhood is an all-consuming passion for her and is something we will never understand. What I do understand is that these pursuits make her intensely happy, and she throws herself into them with a joyful abandon. She has the youth, energy, and life to do it and never turns down the opportunity. I pray that I would follow my passions with the same zeal and enthusiasm. I hope that all of us would never fail to chase after our pursuits with zest and excitement while we are able.

There is so much that we can learn from this little spotted dog of ours. Like many things though, we need to just pause and reflect—searching for insight and wisdom. That, my dear Claire and Wells, is yet another lesson from Lucy.

I love you both so much!
Dad

The Seventh Letter

Fruit of the Spirit

Dear Claire and Wells,

Building a quality or skill into your life is a difficult thing. It requires discipline, patience, and courage. Watching the Olympics this week in London reminds me that these athletes did not come by their prowess without massive effort and practice over the course of decades. You cannot simply plug in and turn on. There is no way to achieve results without sustained effort, in other words, there are no short cuts.

As admirable as the skills of these athletes are, they are not permanent. Physical abilities wither with age, and other athletes inevitably emerge who break records and achieve better results. The things that are permanent are character traits and qualities in our lives that can deepen with age and experience rather than fade away.

You know that your dad reads his Bible every morning, and I constantly am amazed by what I learn. It is new to me every day. Months ago, I was reading Paul's letter to the Galatians. In chapter 5, he discusses the "fruit" of God which he describes as the following: love, joy, peace, patience, kindness, goodness, faithfulness, gentleness, and self-control. Quite a list! I've come to believe that these things are the ultimate and permanent qualities that should be inherent in my life. For these things I will forever strive. As I have begun to really focus on pursuing them, however, I am realizing that they are incredibly difficult to sustain and nurture.

I have also come to realize that the only way to "practice" these qualities is for them to be tested. This is a process that is far from pleasant. For an athlete to improve a skill set, he or she must undergo excruciating and long training. The same holds true for us as we pursue the fruit of the Spirit as Paul describes. Love for example is not increased by simply wishing it so. It must be taxed, stretched, and confronted with hardships for it to expand. The same is true for all of the others. Patience is not simply picked up. In fact, I have found with alarming regularity that when I pray to God to increase my patience, he invariably puts in my path opportunities and people who *test* my patience and force me to practice it!

At the end of the day though, I am coming to realize that the pursuit of the fruit that Paul describes is worth any price. As I am tested also, I am able to gain perspective on *why* certain things happen. In other words, God is using tough circumstances, misfortunes, and heartaches for a greater purpose. The bad things that happen are building in us eternal qualities that cannot otherwise exist. Knowing this helps us get through the rough things in this life.

My dear children, I love you so much. As your father, it is very difficult to see you undergo challenges. I hope that when you do, you will know that it is for the best and that your temporary pain will produce incredible and eternal fruit.

So much love,
Dad

The Eighth Letter

Fear

Dear Claire and Wells,

You know your old man likes to wear out songs. I'll find a few I like
and then listen to them over and over until no one in the family can
take it anymore. The best tunes for me have a driving drum line, an
upbeat melody, and great lyrics. If I find one with all three—look out.

    In the past week or so, I discovered Awolnation's "Kill your
Heroes." While the title seems a bit strange, the music is solid, and
the lyrics are phenomenal. The first verse runs like this:

> Well I met an old man
> dying on a train.
> No more destination,
> no more pain.
> Well he said,
> "one thing, before I graduate…
> never let your fear decide your fate."

    There is some wisdom here for sure. The first thing to point out
is that the retrospective view of the elderly can be incredibly important and insightful. I am always interested in hearing the wisdom of
the aged. As young people, your natural and initial reaction to senior
citizens will likely be impatience and intolerance. They are likely

35

people who do not share your interests or passions and are not participants in the language, trends, and pace of your culture. You must always remember though that these surface issues hide the real value of interacting with seniors—their experience and vision. These are incredibly valuable things! Listen to the elderly. Interact with them!

Back to the lyrics—Aaron Bruno (the lead singer for Awolnation) establishes that he is in fact listening to an older person at the end of his life impart some wisdom. The train setting is important in that it establishes that all of us face the same course: we are on rails with a single destination. In other words, our mortality is shared and irrevocable. "No more destination, no more pain." Great lines indicating that goals require effort and suffering to achieve. The crowning thought from the verse lies, however, in the final line, "never let your fear decide your fate." Now that, Claire and Wells, is a serious bit of wisdom that you should ponder.

Fears are funny little notions that humans pump up into monstrous life changing things. Never listen to them nor give them any credence in your life. If you do, they will hinder you from achieving your goals, stymie your dreams and as Aaron Bruno says, they will dictate your fate.

I know we have kicked around the idea of fear in my letters to you in the past but bear with me a little bit longer. I am reading Andre Agassi's autobiography, _Open_, right now. He is a flawed character (like all of us) but is someone that I grew up watching on the tennis courts. The shocking thing is that he is a very talented writer. Agassi compares fears to gateway drugs. He says that if you give in to the little ones, it won't be long until the bigger ones are ruling your life. How true.

We could spend a ton more time on the rest of this Awolnation song. I find the chorus very intriguing also. Enough for now though. I want you to always remember Paul's writings to his disciple Timothy, "For God has not given us a spirit of fear, but rather of power and of love and of discipline." Kick your fears to the curb. Reach for your dreams and goals. Never let anything decide your fate but your own heart.

Love you so much!
Dad

The Ninth Letter

Kill your Heroes

Dear Claire and Wells,

I could not resist following up on my last letter to you. You probably recall that the Awolnation song "Kill your Heroes" had me mesmerized not only by the music but also due to the surprising lyrical content. Aaron Bruno is probably not the second coming of Aristotle or the possessor of the key to life, but there is clearly inspiration in this catchy tune. As with most songs, interpretation is critical to unlocking meaning, and I am sharing with you my view on what this song is trying to tell us.

Check out the chorus:

> I say you kill your heroes and
> Fly, fly, baby, don't cry.
> No need to worry cause
> Everybody will die.
> Every day we just
> Go, go, baby don't go.
> Don't you worry we
> Love you more than you know.

Amazing indeed are the interests of average people. As an example, the amount of time, energy, and money that gets poured into professional sports is staggering. It is an entertainment industry built to supply armchair excitement to countless souls who for lack of their own passions and drives live vicariously through headlining athletes. I do not condemn the casual intake of games and matches as a recreational diversion; I do seriously wonder though about the danger of idolizing sports figures. In many cases, the star quarterback is lifted up as a hero.

There it is—the first few lines of the chorus are powerful indeed. Bruno is certainly not agitating for the death of true heroes but rather laments the fact that so many of us worship and waste precious time by idolizing people who are in no way important. The thought that we should forget about these people, get off our collective rumps, and chase after our own dreams is aptly summarized. What are your dreams and goals? Are you willing to pursue them with abandon? I so want you both to "fly!"

Moving through the chorus, I especially appreciate the stark reminder of our mortality. Death is the great equalizer. No matter our station in life, level of achievement, wealth or fame, we all face the exact same fate. Given this fact and perspective, I can see the wisdom of not sweating the small stuff. None of us have time to worry or fret about things we cannot control. Additionally, at the end of the day, the rich and famous go out on the same terms as the poor and lowly. So go, go every day, get after your vision, go for your dreams.

Finally, the speaker of this chorus is revealed through the final line. Aaron Bruno (whether by choice or coincidence) is channeling the words of our great God. This chorus is his voice! You see my dear children, there is absolutely no need to worry or fear. There is no reason for anxiety or stress. The God who created the universe wants nothing more than a relationship with you. That God in three persons, the Father, the Son, and the Holy Spirit, the God who set all things in motion loves you more than you know.

I love you too!
Dad

The Tenth Letter

Hope and Faith

Dear Claire and Wells,

Before you were born, Claire, your mother and I spent hours thinking through potential names for you. It was an exciting time for us. We were so looking forward to the birth of our beautiful little firstborn. We bought books of children's names and made lists of possibilities. We even posted our top choices on the refrigerator. I favored for a time the *virtue* names: Faith, Hope, and Grace. My top choice for a few weeks was Hope. It seemed a wonderful name with a nice ring and a rich history. I am so glad now that we chose another name. Hope has become a word and a concept that I truly dislike.

There are clearly proper uses of the word, but they are very few indeed. The heart of the matter is this: the word hope implies that you have no control or influence over your situation or fate. It conveys a sense of powerlessness that leaves you only with room to passively wish that an outcome will be favorable or a dream might come true. When I hear the words "I hope so" uttered, it causes me to cringe. Most of the time, the phrase is used with all innocence. It is simply a conversational refrain bantered about while discussing the weather. In some cases, however, it indicates that the speaker has surrendered and is adrift on the winds of life with no belief or compass.

Let me remind you, Claire and Wells, that dreams can come true and outcomes can be favorable. What is required is only your belief and effort. In other words, your active faith.

Jesus spoke more often about faith than almost any other subject. He healed through faith, required it of His followers, and in one of my favorite lessons indicated that with enough of it—one could move mountains. He never once used the word hope. The concept was not part of his vocabulary, teaching, or worldview. Take a look at this passage from the gospel of Mark:

> In the morning, as they went along, they saw the fig tree withered from the roots. Peter remembered and said to Jesus, "Rabbi, look! The fig tree you cursed has withered!"
>
> "Have faith in God," Jesus answered. Truly, I tell you, if anyone says to this mountain, 'Go, throw yourself into the sea,' and does not doubt in their heart but believes that what they say will happen, it will be done for them. Therefore I tell you, whatever you ask for in prayer, believe that you have received it, and it will be yours.

Hidden in these words is one of the most massive promises made to mankind. The teaching is clear: if you want something in life, it can be yours. Whatever the goal, whatever the outcome, whatever the desire, your faith will bring it to fruition. Not hope. Faith.

The faith required to move mountains is not easily obtained to be sure. It requires focus, determination, and an unrelenting belief. Perhaps it is because of these barriers that so few possess it. Dear children, find and apply this level of faith in your lives. Set your targets high, pray for your intentions, have faith that you will achieve them, and they will be yours. Be unwavering in your faith despite any short-term setback. Know that adverse circumstances that cross your path while in pursuit of your goals are merely temporary and designed to build power and character in your lives. Have the faith to move mountains.

Love you both so much,
Dad

The Eleventh Letter

Complaining

Dear Claire and Wells,

I recently spent some time with a man who for reasons I could never identify is a person whom I regularly avoid. As you know, your old man looks for the best in people, but this is a man who makes that effort a real challenge. There always seems to be darkness surrounding his character and personality that gives me pause, nothing specific, just a feeling. After further time with him a few weeks back, I was able to clarify the issue. This man is a complainer.

The explanation for my dislike may seem a bit simplistic. After all, no one enjoys listening to complaints. However, I have been thinking and reading much about this topic recently, and it has become my belief that the habit of complaining can cause far more serious damage than passing unpleasantness.

Complaining is easy. We are constantly exposed to conditions and circumstances that are not of our choosing. Difficulties and challenges abound and the habit of complaining is a simple one to build. You may notice if you tune your mind to it that most people you interact with will offer some form of complaint in almost every conversation. It might be the weather, an ache or pain, another person, or a personal problem, but it will almost invariably happen. Don't you do it. Not even once. Guard against it with every fiber of your being. The ramifications of going down that road are dangerous indeed.

Here's why: what we focus on expands. When we think about something, we invariably include it in our experience. Thoughts, Claire and Wells, are very powerful and when we complain, we are essentially focusing on the things that we do not want. A complaint draws negativity and darkness into our lives and casts a shadow on those around us. Earlier in this letter I referenced a man whom I have held at arm's length. I now know why. His complaining is causing him to draw negativity towards himself; when I am around him, I can feel his shadow.

As an aside, this man is experiencing all sorts of trouble and has never been successful in any facet of his life. I hope you can see that a complaint, even one that seems casual or small, can be a very destructive and insidious force.

So my dear children, we attract into our lives exactly what we think about. Please get into the habit of focusing only on the best. Learn also to change your response to circumstances. If something does not break your way, look for the lesson and goodness in it. Recognize that what Paul says in Romans 8:28 is always true: "All things work together for good for those who love the Lord." If you can do this, you will draw goodness, light, and incredible success into your lives and into the lives of people around you.

Love you so much!
Dad

The Twelfth Letter

Gratitude

Dear Claire and Wells,

I write this to you from a lounge chair at the beach in Mexico. It is Christmas day, and the weather, sea, and surroundings are magnificent. Your beautiful mother is next to me reading, and I can see your sister, Emma (now ten), splashing in the turquoise surf hunting for sea shells. This is perhaps not the most traditional of Christmas holidays, but it very well could be one of the more relaxing ones. We are making memories by the hour here, and I delight watching your eyes light up, Wells, with the appearance of each buffet, and, Claire, to watch the young Mexican staff swoon over you as you practice your Espanola is a joy. Some may say that this is a very easy place to be grateful in perhaps, but I will tell you that I am filled with gratitude for you, for God's great gifts, and for every single aspect of my life. I have come to believe that constant gratitude and an abiding grateful spirit are one of life's great keys to success.

In a recent letter to you, I addressed the dangers of complaining. Namely, what we focus on expands in our lives and we invariably include it in our experience. You see, my dear children, when we center in on something, we focus energy on it. We concentrate creative and attractive force to it. While this is incredibly damaging when we are complaining or thinking negatively, it is rewarding beyond description when we have a positive and grateful spirit.

Gratitude for all things in our lives causes us to focus on what is good. When we are grateful, we are focusing that same creative and attractive force on the best things in our lives. We know that what we focus on expands and fills us. Gratitude becomes a changing power and will invariably bring peace, happiness, and prosperity to you. You will attract these things into your life. Sound simple? It isn't.

A consistently grateful spirit is a difficult thing to develop. We are constantly exposed to the negativity of the world and of the vast majority of people around us. Additionally, circumstances have an uncanny way of turning out in a very different way than in the manner in which we had planned. We are beset with challenges and sometimes have to deal with intense physical pain (like your old man and his temperamental back). Sometimes we even get terrible messages from those closest to us. Remember Job's *friends*? My point is to work on it. Practice a positive and grateful mind. Look for the good in all things. Work on disciplining your thoughts and giving your attention to only the best. In the words of Paul to the Thessalonians, "In everything give thanks." May your lives be filled with all good things!

Love you both so much,
Dad

The Thirteenth Letter

Radiator

Dear Claire and Wells,

Radiate. Radiant. Radiator. Some words are fun to simply pronounce. They have a sound and vibration aside from their meaning that makes them fascinating. Your dad's favorite poet, Billy Collins, describes this phenomenon best in his poem "Japan:"

> Today I pass the time reading
> A favorite haiku,
> Saying the few words over and over.
> It feels like eating
> The same small, perfect grape
> Again and again.
> I walk through the house reciting it
> And leave its letter falling
> Through the air of every room.

The words radiate, radiant, and radiator produce the same feeling for me. I enjoy the sensation as they come off my tongue and with the repeated saying comes the opportunity to ponder their meaning.

I grew up in houses with radiators. Our oil furnace would heat water in a boiler, and the hot water and steam would course through pipes and flow into cast iron radiators resident in all of the rooms.

These radiators were interesting contraptions designed to maximize surface area so that when the hot steam and water poured through them, they would heat up and (you guessed it) radiate the warmth throughout the area. I never thought much about them. They were just the things that provided us heat in the winter. I guess now that I am aging, my increasing introspection brings new meaning to the mundane.

The radiators in the homes of my youth had no ability by themselves to generate heat or warmth or change in the environment around them. They were completely lifeless and inert. Their designs were different as were their scale and placement, but at the end of the day without the hot water and steam flowing through them, they were nothing. In fact, they were worse than nothing. These old radiators were bulky, unsightly, and obtrusive in a room. You were forced to defer furniture placement around them and decorate with deference to them. However, add the flowing steam and water and they provided warmth, heat, and had the ability to change the environment around them. Claire and Wells—these things are just like us. We are radiators.

People are flawed and at times obtrusive things that take up space and offer no real value on their own. Sometimes we are interesting looking and certainly come in a variety of sizes, but without the Spirit and grace of God flowing through us, we are just inert objects. Add the power of God and we can radiate his life, his love, his warmth—we change the environment that surrounds us. Furthermore, this is what we were created to do. Much like the old cast iron radiators that were designed and constructed to receive and radiate heat, God created us in his image to receive and radiate his awesome life, grace, and warmth to those around us. Finally, we are happiest when we are fulfilling our purpose. As we radiate God's grace and warmth, we are truly at peace.

For old times' sake, go back and listen to a favorite song by Family Force 5 "Radiator" and think of the neat experiences we had together in days gone by. We loved the *crunk* music during our days living in Georgia; now we can reflect in the wisdom of the lyrics.

Think through your own lives, my beloved children, and challenge yourselves to radiate. Be radiant. Be a radiator.

I love you so much!
Dad

The Fourteenth Letter

Wonder

Dear Claire and Wells,

We've lost our sense of wonder, and we don't even know it. The world around us is teeming with magnificence, splendor, and abundance, and we are unable or unwilling to recognize it. Humans are dulled by routine, desensitized by media, boxed in by peers, and focused almost exclusively on themselves. The lenses that we look through are clouded in the extreme, and the result is a gray landscape that holds few surprises and precious little amazement. What a tragedy…

Wells' sixteenth birthday trip out west was incredible. You may remember that when we arrived in Denver, we took a bus ride to pick up our rented car. The most interesting passenger on that bus was a small boy of no more than three years old who spent his time alternatively hanging from the ceiling-mounted handrails or standing in his mother's lap. He was absolutely mesmerized by the bus, the road, the scenery, the motion, and the simple opportunity to be present for the experience. His passion was unchecked, his enthusiasm unbridled, and his zest for life unburdened. He saw a world full of vibrancy and excitement. We need to get back to that state. The state that God intended for us. The state where we can experience awe of his creation and of the simple joys that surround us.

A few years back, I had the opportunity to hike the Grand Canyon with your uncle Bill. We did the entire twenty-six-mile journey from rim to rim in a single day. It was a grueling experience but one that I will never forget. The sheer magnificence of God's creation is so utterly breathtaking that it causes you to question your own purpose and importance. Carved into the rock wall just beneath the South Rim is a verse from Psalm 104. It is a verse that I have long since committed to memory and one that I find myself oft repeating:

> How great are thy works, O Lord!
> In thy wisdom thou has created them all.
> The earth is full of thy riches.

Imagine the impact of this verse while contemplating the Grand Canyon landscape. It is impossible to view such majesty and not become closer to God. The real challenge for us as humans is to not need the prompt of a Grand Canyon experience to gain back our sense of awe and wonder. What we need to possess is the innocence and passion of the three-year-old boy riding in that bus heading to the rental car depot in Denver, Colorado. We need to see splendor in all things and in all situations. We need to get excited!

As with most things in this life, no easy path exists to achieving a worthwhile outcome. We need to work at it. In my own life, I have begun striving to recognize the beauty and opportunity in the mundane and routine. I am looking for God's hand and signature in people, surroundings, and situations. The result of my efforts have been rewarding in the extreme: I am regaining my long lost sense of wonder and awe. The beauty and majesty that has always surrounded me is becoming visible again.

Finally, my dear children, remember that you are always in the right place at the right time. The only question is whether or not you are acting as the right person.

I love you both so much,
Dad

The Fifteenth Letter

Taking Risks

Dear Claire and Wells,

I had an interesting conversation recently with a friend of mine at the University Club. We were visiting over lunch, and the discussion turned to the factors of success. In other words, why does one person achieve great things while another person does not? Clearly, there are many answers to a broad question such as this, but our conversation was very focused. We were comparing business people of similar skill sets, education, intelligence, and background who were operating in the same environment. I cannot recall how we became engaged on this subject, but my friend had a very specific answer that truly resonated with me. Before I share with you his thoughts, I will tell you that this is a very successful man who recently sold one of his companies for a seven-figure sum and has multiple other ventures underway. He is an entrepreneur who keeps his own schedule and answers to no one. As enticing as his current situation may sound, it wasn't always this way for him.

As we talked, he revealed the results of some serious introspection done a few years ago. At the time, he was a corporate executive with a major financial services firm and was by most measures quite successful. He wanted more and realized that he was capable of more. This determined his new path in life and unlocked his belief of what it takes to leapfrog ahead. The key, he surmised, was the willingness to embrace risk. As he surveyed the landscape of those around him, the thought occurred to him that none of the people who had achieved great things were any more talented, intelligent, or skilled than he was. The difference was simply that at some point, they had taken a big risk and chased a dream.

Our conversation reminded me of a survey of which you have probably heard me talk about before. This survey was conducted in nursing homes around the country many years ago. One of the questions posed to the elderly residents was simply, "What are your biggest regrets?" The top answer (predictably) was that the respondents wished that they had spent more time with their families. The number two answer to the same question was the keen wish that these people had taken more risks in their lives. I find that fascinating! What a huge lesson for all of us!

In thinking over my University Club conversation over the last several weeks, I am sure that the assumption of risk is not the sole contributor of achievement nor is it the only differentiator between those who make great things happen and those who do not. However, I have become convinced that it is a huge factor in attaining great things in our lives. Mentally go through all the notable characters in history and you will find the common theme: all of them took significant reputational, financial, or physical risk. More often than not, they took these risks repeatedly. To be sure, the risks taken were always calculated, but the fact remains that achieving great things requires taking great risks.

You will notice as you go through your lives, Claire and Wells, that most people are unwilling to take risk. They prefer to seek security and comfort at every turn. While this is not necessarily a bad thing, the common path will lead to an average life that may hold regrets at its end (remember the nursing home survey). Few of those who shun risk will accomplish anything of significance in their lives. They may be wonderful people with beautiful families, happiness, and good legacies—but will never win the gold medal, contribute greatly, or change their environment.

You both are just now embarking on life's incredible journey and what an adventure awaits you! God has given you both amazing gifts and talents, and I am convinced that he would not want you to squander those gifts by playing small and not striving to become *all* that you can be. Note the lessons from Jesus and all the biblical characters that your dad talks so often about—take risks, strive for great things, and don't play small.

I love you both so much!
Dad

The Sixteenth Letter

Patience

Dear Claire and Wells,

Patience has been a very hard trait for me to acquire. Patience with people, patience with situations, patience with things, patience with results, and patience with circumstances are all challenges that can raise my blood pressure and set my teeth on edge. The apostle Paul talks about the "fruit" of the Spirit in his letter to the Galatians. He lists those characteristics as love, joy, peace, patience, kindness, goodness, faithfulness, gentleness, and self-control. In my humble view, patience is the toughest because it requires the employment of all of the other virtues. In other words, to truly exhibit patience, you must be loving, internally joyful, filled with peace, and have huge self-control. That is a very big requirement especially for a type "A" guy like me. However, I have come to believe that the pursuit of patience is worth the pain and effort.

At the core, losing your patience in a given situation robs you of your personal power. You immediately grant other people or events control over you. Let's run through a mundane example that occurred to me this week and gave me insight into this phenomenon. As you know, I normally take the 6:34 a.m. train from Winnetka to Chicago. It regularly is a few minutes behind schedule but very rarely do things get much worse than that. This week, the rail line lost power to their track switching equipment and shortly before we pulled into the downtown station, the train was forced to stop as repairs were attempted. One thousand passengers sat on that train for over an hour within sight of our destination. I had a tremendously busy morning ahead of me with no room for delays, and it would have been a very easy thing to lose my patience like so many of my fellow passengers. As the minutes rolled by, people around me started to pop off. You could feel and see the tension mount and tempers flare. In the observation of all this came my insight. I watched while people gave away their mornings and productivity to something totally out of their control. In this instance, I was able to focus my energy and get a ton of work done on that stopped train.

You see, Claire and Wells, I have found that there are two necessities that must be present in order to maintain composure and remain patient. The first ingredient is a spirit of gratitude. It might be difficult to see the link, but a grateful spirit allows you to see opportunities in all circumstances and look for the best in all things. Back to the story of my train ordeal, I focused on being grateful for the found time where I could work undisturbed by phones, emails, and colleagues. With gratitude, I then accomplished a great deal. Secondly, I have come to understand that we are all always in the right place at the right time. In my view, God has a master plan and is placing us in circumstances and situations for a reason. Believing this will allow you pause while you are in a moment that is testing your patience. Ask yourself at these times: What can I learn? Who can I meet? How can I offer grace and inspiration to those around me? What can I accomplish? I guarantee you that this will change the way you view any inconvenience.

Additionally, you both know that your father also gets his patience tested while he waits for results. Whether it is business, fitness, performance improvement, or anything else—waiting for results is something that is particularly difficult for me. I suspect that it has something to do with our universal desire for instant gratification, or perhaps it is my own drives and ambitions. Whatever the root cause, waiting for results is a very hard thing. I'll give you another two considerations that may help in this arena. First, striving toward a goal is quite a bit like tending a garden. You can control your effort in terms of weeding, mulching, plowing, planting, and clearing. Your work continues as you fertilize, protect, and water constantly. There comes a time, however, that you must surrender some control over the results of your efforts and trust that the work you have done will bear good fruit. In other words, when the young plant appears, it will truly hurt your efforts if you reach down and start tugging on it to grow at a faster rate than God intended it to. You will only damage things and destroy all your hard work. The same is true when going for a goal. Do everything you possibly can, work as hard as you can, and leave nothing on the table. After you have given all you've got, be patient and trust that the results will come as God intends.

Secondly, it's important to recognize that all great achievement takes time and sustained effort. Great performers in every walk of life—sports figures, musicians, authors, actors, and business people reach greatness only through applied practice over a long period of time. You need to know this, embrace it, and enjoy the process. Having this long view will lead you to a patient spirit as well.

In closing, my dear children, be patient with me. Many of the things that I write about are issues that I have far from mastered. However, know that I love you so much and desperately want the best for you in this life. I hope that my letters to you resonate and are helpful in your journey as they have been helpful to me in their writing.

Love you!
Dad

The Seventeenth Letter

Time

Dear Claire and Wells,

Time is running out.

It progresses inexorably without ceasing and is perhaps the single most powerful force that any of us will ever know. It cannot be changed, altered, or halted and is the great equalizer of all mankind. We are all subject to its might.

As I grow older, I am becoming more aware of the nature of time and am becoming keen to ensure that I employ it wisely. Wasting my time or spending it foolishly is something that I will not abide by any longer. My dear children, I wish that I had recognized the rapid and inescapable progress of time earlier in my life and made this commitment sooner. I can tell you that the clichés regarding time are all correct. As you age, it seems that time increases in pace.

As you are regular readers of my letters, it will come as no surprise that I will offer you my thoughts on the matter of time. I hope that you consider my musings and think through them carefully. Know that they were born and written because of my love for you and not from a need to lecture to you as a parent might. With that being said, this subject is important in the extreme.

It is said that youth is wasted upon the young. The phrase has many meanings and is true in every respect. In the early years of life, we have little concept of vulnerability, mortality, and age. We revel in our physical strength and are unable to grasp the value of our other character aspects. Time is seemingly endless with the promise of another tomorrow sure and certain. In this life stage, entertainment is craved, procrastination is easy, and the merits of applied effort are questioned. The wasting of time is normal and even applauded by peers. Claire and Wells, you need to fight this tendency with all your heart. You need to recognize that your time is limited and not listen to those who want to drag you down or hold you back. Maximize your God-granted time here on this earth by focusing on a few simple things.

Firstly, do not procrastinate and let what can be accomplished or started immediately be put off until another day. Tomorrow is promised to no man, and the price of deferring a task or the pursuit of a goal can be catastrophic in your life. You see, regret is a devastating thing, and the surest path toward lifelong regret is procrastination. If you want something, get after it—now! If you make a decision to change something in your life—begin immediately! Banish regret from your life and get moving toward achievement.

Secondly, rather than spend your time—invest it. Your old man has been in the investment business for a very long time. When clients entrust me with their wealth, I am cognizant of the fact that their resources are limited. It is essential that I am able to provide them a return of their investment otherwise they will end up losing their money. Sounds familiar? These principles are also applicable to time. Your time is limited (much more so than with wealth—you can make more money, but you cannot create additional time), and you must get a return from the time you invest in an activity. Otherwise, you will lose in the business of life. Consider deeply how you invest your time. Will it provide a return for you? Will it be beneficial to you or others in some regard? As an aside, recreation is an important part of life. Please don't think that I am eschewing time invested in entertainment. Isaiah himself said, "Quietness and rest shall be your salvation." Some amount of time engaged in fun activities sharpens your mind, freshens your spirit, and renews your energy.

Finally, when you catch yourself wasting time or spending it foolishly, stop immediately and change what you are doing. Be mindful of your most precious resource and make your days, hours, and minutes count. Now go out there and make something happen.

I love you both very much!
Dad

The Eighteenth Letter

Responsibility

Dear Claire and Wells,

I heard an anecdote recently that has gotten under my skin. The story was recounted during a round of golf with a few business people and seemed fairly innocuous in the telling. Like a splinter or a healing cut, however, I cannot seem to stop scratching at it. The result, of course, is my letter now to you.

I have come to find out that the parable originates as one of Aesop's fables. Following is my version:

> A scorpion and a frog meet on the bank of a stream, and the scorpion asks the frog to carry him across on its back.
>
> The frog asks, "How do I know you won't sting me?"
>
> The scorpion says, "Because if I do, I will die too."
>
> The frog is satisfied, and they set out, but in midstream, the scorpion stings the frog.
>
> The frog feels the onset of paralysis and starts to sink, knowing they both will drown, but has just enough time to gasp "Why?"
>
> The scorpion replies, "I could not help it— it is my nature."

No surprise why this story would bother your old man. The suggestion here is a common one and is a premise that you should wholly and totally reject. The ideas that fate is unchangeable and that the nature of a person is set and unable to be altered are patently untrue. At their best, these arguments are merely fatalistic. More insidiously, however, they represent far darker forces.

First, notice how the scorpion takes no responsibility, rather he blames his inherent nature. This is a common theme in today's world and a very dangerous thing. The bottom line is that all of us are certainly responsible for our actions. We own them all—both good and bad. We have the God-granted power of self-control and are able to exercise it at our command.

Following this line of thought, if you give away responsibility for your actions, you at the same time give away your personal power. The act of shifting blame also is a statement. The statement clearly communicates that there is no personal strength or discipline present and those are, of course, the key ingredients of a successful life. Everyone makes mistakes; in fact, everyone makes big ones. The point is to not become a victim but own your actions, good and bad, and grow from the experiences.

You see Claire and Wells, the reality is very straightforward: you can achieve or become almost anything in life you want if you simply apply enough discipline, desire, hardwork, and faith. There are no unrealistic goals. In fact, I believe a goal or desire would not be present within a person unless they have the means and capabilities to achieve it. However, if you give away your power, you might as well throw in the towel on any pursuit or dream. You will likely achieve very little.

Finally (and very sadly), you will find in your life that most of the people around you would prefer that you achieve little. They would prefer that you drift along in mediocrity—like them. They fear that if you take responsibility for your actions and exercise your personal power, you will accomplish great things. When you do this, it seriously challenges their own comfort, self-worth, and beliefs.

Never accept an excuse from anyone wherein blame is shifted elsewhere or full responsibility is not borne. Hold those around you accountable and hold yourself accountable. Drive forward for great things and always believe in your own power to achieve them.

Love you!
Dad

The Nineteenth Letter

On Death

Dear Claire and Wells,

My friend died last week. He was fifty-two years old.

It happened in the men's locker room at the University Club of Chicago. He mentioned that he was having a hard time catching his breath during his workout, and as he began to ready himself for a shower and a normal workday, he collapsed. Our fellow members worked on him until the paramedics arrived and took over but to no avail. His family is beautiful; his eldest daughter is heading off to her freshman year in college in a few weeks, and his younger daughter will begin her sophomore year in high school. I am grieving for them and am saddened by the sudden loss of a good man.

You will not be surprised to hear that John's passing has been weighing heavily on me. An event like this makes you very mindful of your own mortality and on the fleeting nature of life. Our moments in this world are short indeed and can come to an end quite suddenly. With these thoughts on my mind, my reflections over the past week have brought me to a few personal conclusions.

First, I must guard my time. I have written to you previously on the nature of time, but my friend's death has caused me to hone in on it even further. You see, Claire and Wells, I can get more of just about anything in this life. I can make more money; I can buy another house, boat, car, or any of the other "stuff" that I want. I cannot get more time. Because of this, time is my most precious resource. I need to savor it, invest it wisely and be thoughtful and intentional about where and how I spend it.

Second, I don't want to have regrets. When I am in the sunset of my life, I don't want to feel that things remain undone. At the end of my life, I will not be able to tolerate the phrase, "I wish I had…" The lesson for me is to simply go after the things that I want to have, do the things I want to do, go to the places I want to go, and spend time with people who are important to me.

Third, I need to get after it. By this I mean that it is tremendously important to me that I am striving hard to be the very best man I can be. Whatever my current goals are, I want my efforts to be maximized, and I desire to leave no gas in the tank and no reps on the bench. The famous quotation from Theodore Roosevelt jumps into my mind as I write, and I will repeat it here as it captures my thoughts perfectly.

> It is not the critic who counts; not the man who points out how the strong man stumbles, or where the doer of deeds could have done them better. The credit belongs to the man who is actually in the arena, whose face is marred by dust and sweat and blood; who strives valiantly; who errs, who comes short again and again, because there is no effort without error and shortcoming; but who does actually strive to do the deeds; who knows great enthusiasms, the great devotions; who spends himself in a worthy cause; who at the best knows in the end the triumph of high achievement, and who at the worst, if he fails, at least fails while daring greatly, so that his place shall never be with those cold and timid souls who neither know victory nor defeat.

Fourth, our family is everything to me. I know that we love each other very much, but I also know that we all have different interests, are at different points in our lives, and are seeking different things. This is all natural and healthy. The events of the past week however have reminded me that our family bond is the one consistent thread that we will carry for our entire lives. It is a sustaining power, a wellspring of solace, comfort, and joy. It is quite likely a more powerful force than we have ever realized. As such, we need to treat our family bond like a cherished garden. Let's invest in it, tend to it, and nourish it. I believe it will bear fruit beyond our understanding.

Know this, my dear children: you two along with your mother and beautiful sister are the light of my life and my reason for living. I only hope that my actions always reflect my heart's true feeling.

All my love,
Dad

The Twentieth Letter

Adversity

Dear Claire and Wells,

Adversity will be a constant companion throughout your lives. You will struggle with challenges, deal with setbacks, and be forced to fight for territory at almost every turn. I tell you this not to bring you down but rather to share with you the hidden promises inside each obstacle. You see, my dear children, as difficult and painful as these problems may appear in the moment, they are the vehicles that will allow you to grow yourselves and reach new heights in your life.

When you strive for something, obstacles are immediately set in place. In fact, as your ambitions and dreams grow in scale, you will absolutely find that the magnitude of your challenges will increase almost in direct proportion. While this may seem terrifying at first, understand this—you will not be holding on to a dream or a goal unless you have the capacity within you to achieve it. Take comfort in this and allow it to give you perspective as a problem arises.

It is also essential that you face problems head on and deal with them in a straightforward manner. Most people will avoid confrontation and problems at all costs. They run from conflict and will act always in order to avoid any anticipated discomfort. This type of behavior only leads to stagnation and unhappiness. Unfortunately, these people will never be able to accomplish anything of consequence. They are guaranteeing themselves lives of regret and mediocrity. Don't go down this path. When a problem or adverse situation arises, tackle it.

Important also is the capacity to learn from each obstacle and mistake. These things can be very painful indeed, and there is no need to go through each fire more than once. Build in yourselves an evaluative and reflective nature. In other words, be able to look back over the landscape and examine it with clarity and objectivity. Ask yourself what happened, what you would do differently given similar circumstances, and build this new knowledge into your character. Keep your faith though and remain focused on your objectives. I will tell you that at times, as hard as you look for a lesson in something, it will not be immediately evident. When this happens, keep moving forward with unwavering vision, confidence, and faith.

As you know, I have been reading the book of Isaiah quite a bit recently and have become fascinated with the wisdom and promises contained in the old prophet's writings. No surprise that the Bible is full of references on God's providence and care for us, but I love Isaiah's words in chapter 26. In verse 3, he says: "The steadfast of mind Thou wilt keep in perfect peace, because he trusts in Thee. Trust in the Lord forever, for in God the Lord, we have an everlasting rock." Stay focused on your objectives, and be steadfast of mind. Know that God is a rock for you and a harbor in the storm. Trust that in all things, God's plan is better than yours.

This last week has been fraught with challenges for your dad at work. Two of my team members left; we lost a sizable family relationship; we were informed by a significant potential client that they have selected a competitor instead of our firm, and a transaction that I had worked very hard on for a period of six months ended up being only one fifth of the size that we had expected, dealing a very serious blow to our revenue stream. To be honest, as I reflected back over the week on that Friday afternoon, I felt like a steamroller had gone over me. I cannot remember a more difficult week for our team. As I ponder it now—just a few days later, the blessings are becoming evident. We have capacity for higher caliber professionals now in our group; we have become better at competing for new relationships; we are hungrier to grow our business, and we are more committed than ever to achieve great things. This stuff has done nothing but sharpen my desire, hone my edge, and strengthen my character.

Claire and Wells, I have come to believe that real growth and achievement in life comes only through pushing past pain and navigating tough challenges. Eagles only reach tremendous heights when there is turbulent air, and athletes only improve when they push themselves beyond their limits. Recognize then the gifts inherent in the obstacles you encounter and know that:

> The Lord will continually guide you and satisfy your desire in scorched places, and give strength to your bones; and you will be like a watered garden, a spring of water whose waters do not fail. (Isaiah 58:11)

I love you both more than I can say.
Dad

The
Twenty-First Letter

Getting After It

Dear Claire and Wells,

The Chicago train system is awesome. I can hop on at the station just a few blocks from our home and be downtown in less than thirty minutes. The passenger cars are comfortable, clean, heated in the winter, cooled in the summer, and offer a great place to read or work. The best part is simply not having to drive. The stress of clogged roads and the waste of time is too much for me. Your old man wants no part of sitting in traffic anymore.

In my years of riding on the trains, I have noticed a few very interesting dynamics, one of which I would like to share with you. You both know that the train terminal in Chicago is a big place, full of stores, restaurants, and people. In the morning, there is a bustle and energy present as thousands of people arrive and head off to their work. For the most part, all the riders tend to funnel out toward the business district. That takes them from the platforms, through the great hall, and then down the long east corridor to exit at the river onto Madison Street directly across from the Opera building. The flow and volume of people creates a human wave that snakes along and spills out into Chicago. Here is the interesting part: this human "wave" has tremendously different characteristics and dynamics during different times of the morning.

I generally catch the 6:34 a.m. train which arrives downtown just after 7:00 a.m. At this early hour, the tidal wave of people is full of vibrancy and urgency. The pace is rapid, and individuals stride with a seeming purpose and intent. There is a vitality to the flow that is invigorating to observe and fun to be a part of. The dynamics change as the morning wears on; if I have an early meeting in the suburbs and catch a later train, let's say the 7:48 or 8:43—the volume of people flowing in the terminal will be the same, but the vibrancy and vitality felt is significantly less. The wave moves more slowly, there is less energy, and things seem slightly flat.

I think I have figured out what is going on here. The early crowd is early for a reason—they have a purpose and intent that is driving them toward something. The sense of urgency and vitality is there because of the shared drive that exists. The air of determination and desire to make something happen is observed and felt.

Not so with the crowds arriving later in the morning.

To paraphrase Albert Einstein—people are like bicycles, they only maintain balance if they are going toward something. In other words, we are happiest and most alive when we are in pursuit of a goal or objective. The specifics of the dream or end state matter not. There simply needs to be something for which we are striving. Something that makes us hop out of bed, catch an early train, and hustle. The key, Claire and Wells, is to figure out what it is that fires you up at this point in your life. I would encourage you to think about it, determine what it is, and then head towards it with enthusiasm and energy.

One more thing on this topic, don't listen to people who talk about "taking life as it comes" and "going with the flow." There is nothing inherently wrong with either of those things, but the underlying philosophy is flawed. A life spent simply coasting along is a life that will be full of regret and sorrow at its end. On the other hand, a life spent in the pursuit of dreams and interests is joy-filled and blessed indeed.

Love you both so much!
Dad

The
Twenty-Second Letter

Nehemiah

Dear Claire and Wells,

You know that it has long been my habit to get up early and start my day with prayer and some reading from the Bible. Over the years, I have covered quite a bit of ground in the scriptures and am always amazed that no matter how many times I read a passage, the text always seems fresh and new to me. Recently, a friend mentioned that he had been reading a book in the Old Testament called Nehemiah and that he had taken a few things away from it. I could not recall much about the old prophet so the next morning, I delved into it again. Oh man, was I surprised.

Nehemiah lived in the fifth century BC and appeared at first as a simple servant to one of the great Persian Kings. On the surface, the story seemed fairly straightforward, and I could see why I might have passed through it without a more studied glance. Essentially, Nehemiah left his post as a king's servant, repaired the walls around Jerusalem and then retired. After a number of years, he came back to Jerusalem and found that people had fallen away from following God's law, so he whipped them back into shape. End of story.

There is so much more to it than that. Over the last few weeks, I have read the book a few times and am amazed at the life lessons that are laid out. The things that Nehemiah does, the beliefs that he holds, the values that he espouses are timeless and applicable for all of us in almost any situation.

First, Nehemiah prays before he does anything. The guy essentially gets on his knees and asks for God's help, guidance, and strength prior to making a decision or tackling an issue. This sounds so obvious and reasonable, yet the reality is very few people live this way. I am here to tell you, my dear children, that there are so many times in my life when I have chosen a course of action without any thought to seeking God's wisdom and direction. The God of the universe loves each of us so much and desires to have a relationship with us. Why wouldn't we call on his help? He is waiting to pour out his blessings on us—we just need to pay attention and ask.

The second lesson I took from Nehemiah stemmed from his interaction with his master, the king. Here was a lowly servant who when asked by the king why he looked sad responded by telling him exactly why and then directly asked the king for money, troops, resources, protection, and time. The audacity of his requests was almost beyond understanding. You know what? The king granted him everything. There is an expression in business that is much used—"Ask for the order." Most people are too afraid, timid, or nervous to do so. Take the cue from Nehemiah, make your requests boldly and respectfully of anyone, and you will likely be surprised at the positive response.

Thirdly, Nehemiah had an unshakeable vision. He was absolutely determined to rebuild the walls surrounding the city of Jerusalem and thereby restored the city's security and pride of its people. He faced ridicule, mockery, threats, violence, and all sorts of adversity while in pursuit of his vision. He was absolutely unfazed. At one point, he talked about having to keep weapons in one hand while working so dire was the situation. This type of resolute determination is the only way that dreams and goals get accomplished. You see Claire and Wells, when you go after something, people will automatically try to trip you up or slow you down. Not because they want you to fail (though sometimes they do) but simply because by pursuing a dream, you are challenging their own sense of comfort and belief of what is possible. Don't listen to them. Follow Nehemiah's example.

Finally, Nehemiah was tough and uncompromising in his values and principles. He was a man of high standards, integrity, and character. As an example, he came back into Jerusalem, found out about some corners being cut and ended up beating a few guys into submission. Literally! If I think through the people in my life whom I most respect, they are the ones who hold similar high values and standards. We leave little behind in this life and take nothing with us except for our reputations. Make sure that when people think of you, they first think about your moral compass and character. Don't ever compromise.

Love you both!
Dad

The
Twenty-Third Letter

Believe in Yourself

Dear Claire and Wells,

I am comfortable enough in my own skin to admit to you that *The Matrix* is one of my very favorite movies. This will come as no surprise given that we have talked about it for years, and you are very familiar with my odd cinematic tastes. I know that I am supposed to appreciate "meaningful" or "artistic" movies such as Orson Wells or Alfred Hitchcock directed classics, but at the end of the day, I love the action and slick fight scenes of the big budget modern stuff. What makes *The Matrix* very interesting to me is that it combines some of the best fighting sequences, incredible special effects, and a really neat story. One more thing, believe it or not, the movie is meaningful in the extreme and carries powerful life-changing messages. You mentioned, Wells, that you just finished watching it, and I wonder if you caught its full meaning.

You both know the basic plot line. On a future post-apocalyptic earth, computers have taken over everything and use humans as a sort of power source. We are grown and nourished in a vegetative state in order to produce heat and energy to sustain the machine world. The matrix creates for each person a mental construct that seems real in all respects. Humans feel, think, believe, age, struggle, and live their lives completely in their minds. The true reality is that they are in cocoons existing inside an enormous machine. The hero of the movie, Neo, emerges to expose the matrix and attempts to free the enslaved human race so that they may live a true and free existence. Neo is described as "The One"—a savior.

The conversation around what constitutes reality is the most obvious theme from *The Matrix*. I am reminded by the question from my philosophy classes: "If a tree falls in the woods and no one hears it, how do we know that it made a sound?" Personally, I find these types of contemplations fairly pointless. Back to *The Matrix*, reality is wherever we find ourselves, and we need to make the most of it.

The more intriguing and less obvious theme from the movie centers on the nature and power of belief. Neo harbors within himself questions, desires, and skills that are unexpressed. He takes no action on them and lives a seemingly average life until a group of people recognize his talents, intervene and challenge his complacency. They believe that he has the power and talent to change the world—the question then becomes whether or not Neo has the belief in himself. Through the course of the movie, we watch as Neo's self-belief grows both in strength and conviction. The transformation is staggering. One of the final scenes from the movie is my favorite. After Neo destroys his nemesis, Agent Smith, he breathes deeply, lifts his head, opens his eyes, and as he exhales, he flexes his body and emanates raw power. The world around him bends, shifts, and is distorted by Neo's radiation of strength and force. It is a very cool moment in the movie. Neo's belief in himself has allowed him to fulfill his destiny and becomes everything that he was meant to be.

Claire and Wells, how strong is your belief in yourself?

This movie exposes one of the central tenets of success in life or in any endeavor and that is simply an unshakable self-belief. Neo was nothing until he came into this understanding. Once he grasped it, there was nothing that he could not conquer. The very same rules apply for us. If we believe in ourselves and apply effort over time with an understanding that the outcome is certain, there is absolutely nothing that we cannot achieve. A poem that summarizes this theme very nicely was penned back in 1905. Although the author is disputed, his message is timeless:

> If you think you're beaten, you are. If you think you dare not, you don't. If you'd like to win, but think you can't, It's almost a cinch you won't.
>
> If you think you'll lose, you've lost. For out in the world we find, Success begins with a fellow's will, It's all a state of mind.
>
> If you think you're out-classed, you are; You've got to think high to rise. You've got to be sure of yourself, If you ever want to obtain a prize.
>
> Life's battles do not always go, to the stronger or faster man. But, sooner or later, the man who wins, is the man who thinks he can.

I'll leave you with one final thought from *The Matrix*. Neo's belief in himself was not automatic. It took encouragement and those surrounding him to wake him up to his ability. I hope that I have done enough to have you recognize that you have incredible power and the opportunity to do anything in life that you want. Believe in yourself, dear ones, I most certainly do.

Love you both so much.
Dad

The
Twenty-Fourth Letter

Self-reflection

Dear Claire and Wells,

The weeks leading up to Christmas this year have been absolutely magnificent here in Chicago. The city has been radiant in the wintry white weather with the lights sparkling and the hustle and warmth of the season. Waking up this morning to a fresh coat of snow in the trees has made me so grateful for the blessings of our family and for the place in which we live. I am especially thankful this Christmas for you, Claire, and for your time home with us during your freshman year in college. You are a beautiful young woman in every way, and I treasure our moments together. I am mindful also that they are becoming less frequent...

I have struggled during the holidays so far to have some time for introspection and the search for direction as we head into a new year. You both know how busy I have been at my work recently and with the other projects that are on our family's radar. The noise and press have been overpowering although quite invigorating. Finally, what gives me pause is the small sculpture of St. Joseph in our office here at home. You may remember that I served on the board of directors for a charitable organization here in Chicago called St. Joseph Services. There were wonderful people involved with great hearts and a desire to create better futures for kids in very tough spots. I am forever grateful for my time there and especially thankful for the gift of this small sculpture received from the executive director as my term ended. It reminds me of my path as a father and also invites me to reflect on the values and life of the man whom God chose to raise the Christ-child. I could probably write ten letters to you on what I have learned from Joseph, but today I have been thinking predominantly about how Joseph responded to the promptings of God.

In the Christmas story, we hear that God provides direction to Joseph through his dreams. On three separate occasions, Joseph receives instructions on steps to take that change not only the outcome for him and his family but also the entire course of human history. What is remarkable to me is that Joseph did not hesitate, he did not doubt, he did not question, and he did not deliberate. He did not heed the likely onslaught of negative attention, jeering, and remonstrance. He took action—pure and straightforward.

Unquestionably, Joseph was a man of deep faith and conviction. When reading about these events, most people tend to leave the discussion there. I believe there is a greater lesson. When we read and hear these stories time after time, we tend to think about the characters involved as actors in some sort of scripted drama. We need to understand that these were real people exactly like us. They faced fears, doubts, anxieties, and heartaches in the same way that we do. Knowing this, Joseph's actions are even more interesting. You see, my dear children, Joseph was willing to fully commit to a radical course of action on the promptings of a mere dream. He was willing to suffer disgrace, hardship, and uncertainty because he alone felt moved to do so. His belief in himself and his unwavering faith changed the world forever.

Dreams, ideas, and inclinations have a shelf life, and they must be explored and acted upon immediately. One of the great tragedies of humanity is that most people ignore the "still small voice" guiding them. They may perceive the path to be too hard or are afraid that their actions will be met with ridicule and embarrassment. Worse yet, they may let themselves be talked out of pursuing their dreams by naysayers who lack faith and vision. Imagine if this happened to Joseph.

I pray that you both would have quiet and perceptive spirits open to divine direction. I pray that you would always be willing to act on your dreams despite uncertainty and ridicule, and may you never experience the regret of what could have been.

I love you both so much!
Dad

The
Twenty-Fifth Letter

Keeping your Word

Dear Claire and Wells,

The business world runs on email. It is by far the most prevalent form of interaction between people and between firms and, I would imagine, is rapidly outpacing the telephone as the single most important communication tool for professionals. In a way, this is a sad occurrence in that email traffic does not foster the formation of deep relationships. It does, however, allow for lightning fast input and output and has driven productivity in a global business environment.

Almost all the emails that I receive in any given workday (and that can be several hundred) have an auto-signature at the footer. This preprogrammed content is a real time saver for business people and usually contains the standard fare of name, title, business, and contact information. Your dad's auto signature has all of the above along with a link to my team website and a disclaimer from our firm. Some people customize their footers even more to include testimonials, client lists, and logo graphics. Occasionally, you will see a phrase or motto of some sort. While I generally find this somewhat hokey, we have a family friend who has a very short Latin phrase following his contact information. He is a good and solid man by the way and that fact makes the short phrase intriguing indeed. It reads "Dictum

Meum Pactum"—My word is my bond. While it may not sound like much, there's an awful lot of importance in this old phrase.

Dave Thomas was the founder of Wendy's, the fast food hamburger chain. He was a very principled guy with a strong faith and solid values. One of my favorite quotations of his is the famous "There's no luggage racks on a hearse" expression. We all strive very hard in this life to achieve our dreams and goals and that by the way is a very good thing. Thomas knew, however, that all of our worldly accomplishments would remain here after our deaths. We take nothing from this world with us, and all the things that we accumulate get scattered to the winds. We can leave behind a lasting legacy though—the legacy of a good name and a good reputation. In my view, the fastest route to that legacy is by making sure that your word is your bond. When you say you are going to do something, those who hear you say it should be able to bank on it happening. If you have doubts about your abilities to move forward with something, don't say anything about it until your doubts are gone or you decide to pass on it. Deliver on your promises and honor your commitments. Always.

Claire and Wells, there's another important element here that few think about. Hear me on this. When you keep your word and follow through on the things that you say you will do, you build an incredible belief in yourself. Self-confidence will become like a river within you. Not only self-confidence but also a strong self-belief. A belief that whatever you set your mind to will be achieved. In essence, you train yourself to speak things into existence. The power that comes from a mindset like this is tremendous. If you say that something will be done—it is done.

One more thing, you will find in your lives that the single most important building block in any relationship is trust. It matters not whether it is a business relationship, a friendship, or a love interest. Trust will be the foundation. By the way, the way to build trust with people is to mean what you say, follow through on your promises, and have your word be your bond.

"Dictum Meum Pactum," dear children. For my part, I pledge to pray for you always. I will not stop loving you, caring for you, and thinking about you. I will protect you and strive to act in your best interests at all times. I will be your father in every sense of the word. You can count on it.

With all my love,
Dad

The
Twenty-Sixth Letter

True Strength

Dear Claire and Wells,

You both know that I started reading the Bible when I was your age. I was selective and sporadic in my reading, usually ending up in Proverbs or Paul's letters to the early churches. I liked the wisdom of Solomon outlined in Proverbs and was hoping that some of it might rub off. As for Paul's letters, most of them were fairly short and straightforward, and I did not feel intimidated when I opened most of them. At the time, I avoided most of the Old Testament. I found many of the books there to be boring, cumbersome to get through, or irrelevant to my life. As an aside, I could not have been more wrong. Nowadays, I find a freshness and inspiration in every single book of the Bible. My reading back then was not a daily thing, but I enjoyed it in small doses and felt that it added to my life somehow.

My mother was far more consistent in her Bible reading than I and was typically leading or involved with a number of study groups. She was and remains now a great example to me in the way she pursues her faith. My mom was constantly encouraging me to read Paul's letters to Timothy. On the surface, it made perfect sense. Timothy was a young man, new in his faith and subject to the very same pressures as I was at the time. As a matter of fact, these pressures are the ones you are facing now in your lives. You know them well—the pressure to perform, the pressure to fit in, to be liked, to be intelligent, to be athletic. These types of things have always been there. Sometimes we fall into the habit of believing that the pressures and feelings we have are unique to us. We think that our challenges, troubles, and conflicts are ours alone. Nothing could be farther from the truth. Your mother and I faced the same struggles and pressures that you are now facing as did Timothy and every single other young person in history.

While it then made perfect sense for me to relate to Paul's letters to Timothy, I just could not do it. I read the letters through quite a few times and remember trying to like them and trying to engage with them but to no avail. I viewed Timothy as a sort of weakling. I could not shake the belief that he was a timid guy—bookish, nerdy, and sickly. At one point, Paul writes for him to "use a little wine for the sake of your stomach and your frequent ailments." Remember my perspective: I know I have told you that when I was your age, my identity was completely wrapped up in sports. I was the captain of the football and lacrosse teams in high school and had a good bit of self-conceit. Looking back at it now, I realized that my values were completely off base, and my view of what was important was dead wrong. By the way, I was dead wrong about Timothy also. I know now that strength has nothing to do with the physical realm. Strength is a forged element of your character. It is a virtue built from beliefs, disciplines, and pain. All the great people in history had it and so did Timothy.

Timothy and Paul were very close and jointly involved in spreading the news of Christianity throughout the known world. They were fearless, faithful, and shared the bond of an unshakable faith and a higher purpose. It is quite possible that without these two men, the teachings of Christ would have remained isolated and relevant to only a very small region. Whatever timidity or sickliness Timothy had, he overcame it to change the face of the world. Now that, Claire and Wells, is strength.

Paul wrote to Timothy in his first letter, "Let no one look down on your youthfulness, but rather in speech, conduct, love, faith, and purity, show yourself an example…" I know this can be supremely difficult when met by the massive peer pressures I mentioned earlier, but I need you to think about the consequences. Timothy embraced these values, swam against the current, and changed the course of humanity.

This type of power and impact resides in you both. It resides in all of us. We just need to raise our vision and focus on things that are greater than ourselves, greater than our current circumstances, and greater than the trivialities of our daily lives. Paul wrote in his second letter to Timothy, "For God has not given us a spirit of timidity, but of power and love and discipline." May you recognize the ringing truth in these words, dear children, and like Timothy gain real strength—the strength to change outcomes.

Love you both!
Dad

The
Twenty-Seventh Letter

Vision

Dear Claire and Wells,

I am so grateful that all five of us have the incredible gift of near perfect eyesight. The physical complexity of our eyes is amazing and something that I am not able to fully understand. It is enough for me to simply be mindful of how blessed I am to possess this sense and try to never take it for granted.

Despite the uniformity of the human eye and the physical construction of our bodies, I am always struck by the variation in how people perceive the things that are in their view. The reality is that we all "see" things differently. If you ask two people to simply describe their surroundings, you will likely get two very distinct answers. The individual responses will be colored by their worldview, their state of mind, and their attitude. Let me tell you from experience that things are much more beautiful and fulfilling in life if we "see" them correctly.

You both probably remember that a few years ago, I traveled to the Grand Canyon for the Rim-to-Rim hike. It was quite an adventure. We started at the North Rim lodge, hit the trail head around 5:00 a.m., hiked twenty-five-plus miles or so into the Canyon, past the Phantom Ranch, over the Colorado River, up past Indian

Gardens, and emerged at the El Tovar on the South Rim at around 3:00 p.m. When I stood on the rim of that Canyon, the immensity and greatness of it changed me somehow. It is difficult to describe, but I will say that I saw the power of God laid out in a panorama that took my breath away.

Just a few hundred yards down the trail from the South Rim of the Canyon, an unknown scribe has carved into the solid rock one of my favorite verses from the Psalms of David. "How great are thy works, Oh Lord. In thy wisdom, thou hast made them all. The earth is full of thy riches." The words captured exactly the impact of the view. It was awesome.

Here's the interesting part. Surrounding me were all kinds of people who in the midst of grandeur, saw things very differently. I heard complaints about the heat, the dust, and the effort required. I heard conversations around the length of the drive necessary to visit the Canyon and discussions around every other facet of the day with the exception of the magnificence in front of us. You see, Claire and Wells, most people go through their lives focused only on themselves. They look inward and with this narrow view miss out on the most amazing things. Where is your focus as you go through your everyday life? What do you see?

One more thing on "seeing"... About a year ago, I wrote to you about adversity. You know full well by now that you will come across plenty of stumbling blocks in your lives, some of which will be tremendously difficult for you to get through. I need you to "see" difficult differently from now on. Remember always that there is no progress without struggle, and when adversity crosses your path, I want you to see it as an opportunity to advance, an opportunity to grow, and an opportunity to become the very best that you can become.

I am finishing this letter to you on an airplane, and the view out of my window is getting better by the minute. We are winging our way together toward the Dominican Republic for spring break. After a brutal winter, we are so excited for warm sun and sand, a crystal clear Caribbean Sea, and blessed time together. On this trip, I want you both to look outward with fresh eyes. If you look hard enough,

I can assure you that you will see the hand of God in your surroundings and in each other.

All my love,
Dad

The Twenty-Eighth Letter

Making Memories

Dear Claire and Wells,

Just this week, I was walking home from the train station after work and thinking about the beautiful area in which we live. It has been a chilly spring, but even with the delay in warm temperatures, you can see and feel the change coming. The grass is a vibrant color, and the first flowers are beginning to appear. Our village is a remarkable place, and I am very grateful that we are able to live here. As I walked along, I spied a strong-looking blond teenager playing Frisbee in the park with a young girl with long blond hair. They were having a wonderful time together, and their laughter could be heard from a great distance. The Frisbee tosses would invariably evolve into a game of keep away followed by a wrestling match and gleeful peels from the little one. It was an amazing thing to watch, and I almost shed tears of joy when I realized that it was you, Wells, playing with your little sister, Emma. I ditched the briefcase on the grass and joined the fray until dusk and cold sent us all home.

Oh my, are we blessed… As I thought this week about our time together in the park, other memories of our family began to flood through me. The places we have lived, our travels, our experiences, and our time together. You are everything to me, and the memories that we have created together are the source of indescribable joy.

Now you have heard me talk about goals and objectives for your entire lives. I want to tell you today that memories are even more powerful. You see, Claire and Wells, many times, memories are simply hopes and dreams realized. They can be created and then cherished forever.

For the most part, memories are constructed and built. They are the results of intentional effort and thoughtful preparation applied sometimes over the course of years. When I came across you playing with your sister in the park, Wells, it was more than a random occurrence. Your mom and I chose this community for our family; we worked hard to be able to afford the costs; we poured our values into you and prayed daily for you. It has always been important to us that our beautiful children would love each other and enjoy spending time with each other. When I watched your loving interaction with Emma, I saw my hopes and dreams realized. I saw God's blessing unfold and give me a memory that I will carry with me until the day that I pass on.

There is a second necessary ingredient needed for the creation of beautiful memories. That ingredient is a decision.

As we go through our days, it is an easy thing for us to allow our feelings to drive how we respond, react, and then move forward. If we feel tired, selfish, irritated, or annoyed, we might end up passing on the invitation to make a powerful and lasting memory. Wells, I am sure that when you went to the park with Emma that day, you were exhausted from your training run, hungry, and probably had piles of homework on your plate. Your decision to ignore your feelings and focus instead on your little sister gave all three of us an incredible gift—a gift that we will all cherish for years.

You have heard me tell you that people are creators. We create our own lives, our own destinies, and we certainly can create amazing memories. To author yours, start by being intentional and define what memories you want to have. Secondly, make decisions that will put you in the paths of making those lifelong memories. Seek, my children, and you will find.

Love you so much!
Dad

The
Twenty-Ninth Letter

Momentum

Dear Claire and Wells,

Last week, your mother and I went off to attend my high school reunion in Michigan. It was a great experience and a ton of fun to reconnect with old friends. The years have been kind to some and unkind to others, but for the most part, the weekend was a joyful one.

You know your old man well enough to know that I will seek out a gym or fitness center wherever I am or whatever the occasion. Late Saturday afternoon found me on an elliptical trainer at a brand new LA Fitness in Harper Woods, Michigan. I snapped on the integrated television and was happy to find Notre Dame playing Albany in the Quarter finals of the Collegiate Lacrosse Tournament. Even after all this time, I still get a kick out of watching lacrosse, and it brings back the glory days of your dad's own high school and college exploits. The speed of the game is unbelievable now, and it's a very different sport than it was when I played. As I ground through my workout, I watched something interesting unfold between two very good teams.

When I turned on the game, it was deep into the fourth quarter, and Albany held a three-goal lead. A few more minutes went by and Albany scored twice more in incredible fashion. Albany's offense was led by two Native American brothers who are wizards on the field. Their speed and athleticism leaves you openmouthed, and the pace of their shots is off the charts. With precious few minutes left, Notre Dame was down 12–7. The crowd knew the game was over, the television commentators knew the game was over, and Albany knew the game was over. Here's the thing: they were all wrong. Notre Dame won in overtime in one of the most remarkable comebacks in lacrosse history.

Watching this game unfold reinforced a few core beliefs that I hold. The first one is simply that the power of a belief is virtually insurmountable. You see, Claire and Wells, that Notre Dame team never lost their belief in themselves or their ability. Despite huge odds against them, they were certain that they were going to win that lacrosse game. That unshakable belief caused them to overcome a game clock running out, a powerful opponent, and an entire stadium of naysayers who didn't think they stood a chance. If you believe in yourself and want something badly enough, there is nothing you cannot accomplish.

I also gained a deeper understanding of the key ingredients of momentum. I am certain that you both have studied the scientific components of momentum, but the game reminded me of a few simpler aspects of how the concept actually works in life. Albany's lacrosse team had serious momentum in their favor in the second half of that lacrosse game. The team was on a roll and seemed unstoppable. When the lead stretched to five goals, it almost appeared that they were scoring at will. Those two brothers were carving up Notre Dame's defense.

After that supposedly insurmountable lead was achieved, the Albany team put things on cruise control and started to coast. They started to watch the clock and mentally were celebrating the victory. Notre Dame scored. Then they scored again. Then again. Then again. The momentum of the game changed in the blink of an eye, and all of a sudden, Albany was in serious trouble. The momentum owned by that Albany team was handed to Notre Dame in a power transfer so complete that it was like emptying a full glass of water into an empty one.

Claire and Wells, if momentum is on your side with something, you need to push it. Never let yourself get overly confident or relaxed when you are on a roll. That is the time when you need to work harder, apply more effort, and put your foot down hard on the accelerator. There is an expression in gambling used when someone is on a hot streak. The saying is "Press your Bets." I like it.

Finally, when the momentum is against you and you are down, recognize that it is only a temporary thing. Stick to your beliefs, keep your heads up, stay positive, tune out the naysayers, and be relentless in your work ethic. The tide will turn in an instant, and you will end up as huge winners.

Love you both so much!
Dad

The Thirtieth Letter

Graduation

Dear Claire and Wells,

Just a few weeks ago, I was sitting in a packed field house watching the graduating class of 2014 receive their high school diplomas. Your mother and I had a great vantage point seated high up in the bleachers looking down at over a thousand excited seniors seated on the floor of the arena. We are so proud of you, Wells, and were stuck by the sudden proximity of your departure at the end of the summer. You have made great choices in your high school career, son, and I pray daily that God will give you direction and wisdom in all the choices that you and Claire make going forward. Some of the decisions you make may seem trivial or insignificant at the time, but the reality is that they are cumulative. In other words, for better or worse, we are a product of our choices.

As I sat up in those bleachers looking down at the sea of white adorned graduates, I thought about the varied paths that each one of them will take. Along with my elevated perspective in the field house, I also was looking through the lens of years and experience. I recognized that some of these kids will have early success through their hard work or even luck, some will start off weak but end very strong, some will be consumed with trouble or strife, some will waste their talents with laziness or inertia, and some will even be caught up in illegal activity. Each path taken will be the result of choices made.

What choices will you make, Claire and Wells? How will you make them?

We've talked before about making choices and that seemingly in any given situation, the best choice to make for the long-term is invariably the one that is most unpleasant in the short-term. The examples of this strange conundrum are everywhere, and we face them daily—exercising or relaxing, eating fruit or ice cream, studying or watching television, working or procrastinating. Some are not as obvious but invaluable in the long run such as saying no to social experimentation that many in our world see as a rite of passage, not standing up for your beliefs in a crowd, and not cutting corners in your life. These kind of choices can have devastating long-term consequences. Making the right or harder choices obviously lead to immense long-term rewards.

I am not saying that a bit of rest and relaxation is unhealthy, the reverse is true. Everything has its place and time. I am saying that consistent, correct long-term choices will set you up for huge success in life if you will put up with a little near-term sacrifice. By the way, you will find that few people take this road. It is the path less traveled and great achievers always walk on it.

Understand also that consistent actions form habits both for better and for worse. In other words, when people start making bad (or good) choices, it becomes grooved into them and ingrained into their lives. This fact can be either damaging or rewarding. You probably can see this effect in your own lives already. Make sure that you recognize it. Don't be discouraged if you find yourself caught in a bad cycle though. The amazing gift of free will always exist for us, and we can change our ways at any time. If you get knocked off your horse, make sure you get right back on it. Respond to failure with recommitment; don't get caught in downward spirals and make sure that your renewed resolve is always paired with right and immediate actions.

All these thoughts were flowing through my mind as I watched graduate after graduate walk up to that stage and receive their high school diploma. As each name was announced and each picture taken, it marked the beginning of a timeline that will be governed by choices made. You were one of those graduates, Wells. Your timeline has started, and the book of your life has yet to be written. You hold the pen, and your choices will be the ink.

Love you both so much!
Dad

The
Thirty-First Letter

Pressure and Time

Dear Claire and Wells,

The Chicago to Mackinac Island sailboat race is an event that I dearly love and very much look forward to every year. Everything about the race captivates me, and this year featured a record number of competing boats. This was the one hundred and sixth running and you could absolutely feel the history and traditions hanging in the air throughout the week. The parties and buzz leading up to the start were incredible with the Chicago Yacht Club basin filled with sailors, envious spectators, banners, and a forest of masts laden with pennants and flags waving in the lake breezes.

The race itself was also a ton of fun with a great crew, a great boat, and great weather. It took us about forty-seven hours or so to finish, and the island held the same vibrant scene as was present in Chicago. Your mom and Emma met me on the dock, and we spent two glorious days on the island reveling in the electric atmosphere created by the regatta. Knowing that our boat did not do particularly well in the standings led me to virtually ignore most of the results. It was several days later before I focused on identifying the winning boats and was really intrigued by what I discovered. Remember that this is a race with over three hundred boats, over a distance of three hundred miles within a lake that is big enough to have multiple weather systems going at the same time. Even with all these variables, *the same boats tend to win year after year.*

When you listen to the conversations at all the post-race parties, it typically centers in on the weather, tactics, and decisions made. You hear the word "luck" used quite a bit by those who were not award winners. I know better. The skippers and crew of the top finishers are well-known in the sailing community. They are the ones who work on their boats during the winter months, meet in the cold off season to discuss tactics and strategy, invest in technology and cutting edge equipment, read voraciously, and study their competition. They travel to regattas in Florida or the Virgin Islands and think deeply and consistently about being the best. They leave nothing to chance.

You see, Claire and Wells, consistent top performance in sailboat racing is no different than consistent top performance in anything. People who perform at the highest levels are deadly serious about their craft; they are committed to success despite high costs and are relentless in their desire to improve.

One of the most popular segments on television is ESPN's "*Top Ten*" featured in their Sports Center program. It shows short clips of athletes doing spectacular feats or producing unbelievable plays. The camera catches them in that single moment of glory, and it is an amazing thing to watch. What we don't see and rarely consider is the amount of work, time, excruciating effort, and years of practice that are necessary for these athletes to go through before they ever make it to the highlight reels. Greatness always comes with a price.

You probably remember me telling you that pressure and time are two of the most powerful forces in the universe. When those two things are combined, they unfailingly produce massive change. Think about how a constant drip or flow of water can carve channels and grooves into solid rock or how marble steps in old buildings show depressions from centuries of use.

Here is a promise that is a simple one yet incredibly powerful. If you apply steady pressure over time into something through effort, hard work, practice, and discipline, your results will be consistently phenomenal—guaranteed. Just like those sailors who win the races year in and year out and just like those athletes who are always featured on the highlight films. All it takes is pressure and time.

Love you both so much!
Dad

The
Thirty-Second Letter

Found Time

Dear Claire and Wells,

A few weeks ago, I left the house heading to a client appointment at a popular chain restaurant location in a town a little more than an hour away. As usual, I had researched the route to ensure things went smoothly and that I would be punctual. Not only did the car's navigation system inexplicably take me well off the mark, but I also had the wrong restaurant. After all the dust settled, I was forty-five minutes late and stressed. You know that after twenty-one years with a Swiss Bank, being late for things makes my head spin.

The meeting was fine with a very gracious client, and after we parted, I felt better and started to focus on an incredibly busy day ahead back in the city. Heading out into the sultry day, I opened up the car, put my briefcase in the back seat, hung my suit coat on a hanger, and closed the rear door. Suddenly, the car started its locking sequence, and I watched in disbelief as the mirrors retracted, the security system armed, and the locks clicked home. You both know my car—the thing will not lock you out if you have the key fob nearby and that key fob was (as usual) in my suit coat now hanging untouchable in the back seat of that car. I stared at it for a minute and then tried all the doors unsuccessfully. There was no explanation handy for this one, and I realized that locked in the car along with the key was my wallet, cell phone, laptop computer, and everything else save for a plastic cup of water brought out from the restaurant.

After begging the restaurant manager for extensive use of his phone, I found myself back in the parking lot with a good deal of unexpected and unallocated time. The resolution would take several hours to unfold. Here's the interesting part: that huge headache turned into a massive blessing. I consciously chose to not be frustrated but rather seek God's intent in the situation. The answer came as clearly and plainly as the words written on this page. I was to use this time in prayer for you.

For the next two hours, I paced the adjacent parking lot and prayed deeply for you both. Claire, my dear first born, I prayed that God would bless your industrious spirit and make his path clear for you. He has blessed you with keen intelligence, beauty, and determination, and I know that there is absolutely nothing that you cannot accomplish if you set your mind on it. I begged him to fill you with his grace and love and walk closely with you as you begin your second year of college. I also prayed that he would raise up a husband for you (in due time!) that would cherish you as I do and be a soul mate, provider, and best friend.

Wells, my only son, I prayed for your freshman year in college. It is the first time that we will be apart for any length of time, and it will be very difficult for your mother and me. God has given you a kind and gentle spirit, full of goodness and love. You are a remarkable and solid man with a steady character, tremendous strength, and a razor-sharp mind. I am so proud of you for taking on the Honors in Electrical Engineering major—it is something that I never could have done. During my pacing in that parking lot, I pleaded that God would give you a group of friends that share your values and integrity. I asked that you would be filled with his wisdom in order to determine priorities and his discipline to handle a tough curriculum.

And for you both, I asked that God would walk closely with you and be powerful and present for you at all times as he has been for me.

So deep was I in prayer that it took me some time to notice the puzzled-looking Jaguar technician standing next to my car. The fix was made eventually, and I was on my way—incredibly grateful to God for the gift that he had given me. I hope that all of us will be able to recognize gifts like this that come in often unrecognizable packages. I also hope that we will always be wise in using unallocated time.

Finally, my dear children, know that I love you more than words can express and know that my prayers for you that day were not an unusual occurrence. I pray for you both every single day and will do so until God calls me home.

Love always,
Dad

The
Thirty-Third Letter

The Family Fortress

Dear Claire and Wells,

The house has been very different this month now that the two of you have left for college. Your mother and I alternate between feeling melancholy about your absence and then joyful as we celebrate your accomplishments and independence. Your horizons are so bright.

When you come home this Thanksgiving, you will find older photographs framed and scattered around the house. Wells at age three with a blue sweater, impossibly blond hair, and an inquisitive expression. Claire with a gleeful smile and arms wrapped around magnolia branches almost twenty feet from the ground. Both of you at the hospital welcoming your little sister, Emma, into the world, your hands reaching out and touching her as if you were her guardians. I find myself staring at these pictures daily and thinking of you both. I miss you…

Claire, you turn twenty this month, and the thought astonishes me. You have grown rapidly into a beautiful woman, and I am so proud that you are my daughter. I have always intended to cease writing these letters to you as your teenage years conclude. I simply cannot believe that the day now is upon us. I am mindful that my influence and voice in your life will become more muted as you age and that your attention will be rightly drawn to your future. This is the natural order and one that I will not resist. My role for you is changing now, and as your ship launches, I hope (as all fathers do) that I have helped you build a sound boat, able to withstand stormy seas, and sail fast and true in fair weather.

It is tempting for me as I write to spend time reminiscing about the incredible memories that we have made together. I will spare you of that indulgence and simply say that our family is everything to me and always will be. Going forward, we will need to work on ensuring that the five of us always have that unbreakable love and reliance despite distances or interests. Let's never be separated when we are apart, distracted when we are together, or unkind when we differ. Let's make sure that our family is ever an impregnable fortress of love and support.

You are well used to my sailing analogies by now and know that I just can't help using them. I spend a good bit of time on the helm when I am racing. I love doing it, and it is something that I do well. It requires a serious amount of concentration and a constant evaluation of variables including wind speed and angle, wave action, sail trim, direction, tactics, and an eye toward other boats on the water. A good racing crew is typically a highly functioning team with great skill sets and constant communication. They feed the helmsman information and keep the boat moving fast toward the mark. When it's time for a new helmsman to take over, it is usually a coordinated effort. The new driver will come back to the wheel and shadow the current one. There will be a good discussion about conditions, objectives, and risks along with thoughts on what's ahead. When the actual switch occurs, the change is announced to the crew, and the retiring driver affirms by saying to his replacement, "The helm is yours." Finally, the retiring helmsman stands by the new one for a time to ensure a great transition and to help with questions or adjustments as the driver acclimates to the boat and seas.

Claire, at age twenty, I am telling you that the helm is yours. I will be there right next to you for as long as you need me to be as you acclimate to the wind and water. I have absolutely no doubt that you will be a great helmsman—a much better one than me.

Love you both so much!
Dad

The
Thirty-Fourth Letter

Self-confidence

Dear Wells,

It was just a few weeks ago when we were together for family weekend at the University of Delaware. I will never forget seeing you on that Main Street for the first time as a college student. You looked fantastic, son, and I am so proud of you. It wasn't necessarily the outfit you had, your haircut, or your athletic physique—it was rather a certain look in your eye. Your expression and the way in which you carried yourself conveyed a clear message. It was a message of confidence. It was a statement that clearly said, "I can handle this." Even more than that, you told me that day without saying a word that you can handle anything. You have an aura of self-confidence in you now that is very special. It is a quiet confidence and not a brash one. It is something that if you continue to build correctly, will take you to places that few people will ever go.

Confidence in oneself can be a very fleeting and tenuous quality unless it is laid upon a solid foundation and built slowly over time. It is typically a character trait that is earned and not bestowed. Fought for rather than granted. Without thinking about it, you have been taking steps for years to build a base of confidence in your life. Your mother and I have watched you closely over the years and have treasured your accomplishments. We have watched how you responded to our family's moves from Raleigh to Atlanta to Chicago. We saw how you overcame setbacks with friendships and dealt with challenges on the sports fields. We observed how you tackled projects of your own design and marveled at your innate ability to solve problems. We were so proud that your cross-country peers elected you as a leader. We knew that each of these things was building a solid wall of confidence in your life, one brick at a time.

You already know, Wells, that the steps needed to build confidence can sometimes come at a price. It was painful to go through our moves as a family. We were torn from relationships and friends. The occasional setbacks you have had with various projects and the frustration around striving for goals and having them seem always out of reach was very hard. I think sometimes about the words of Isaiah in chapter 30 when he talks about God giving us the bread of adversity and the water of affliction. The things we go through sometimes are tough indeed, but God knows that it is only through these things that we can reach our potential. It is the food that makes us strong. It is a hard thing to welcome challenges but helpful to know during the pain that you will be in a better place when it is over.

Another interesting thing about confidence is the fact that it is a trait that you can grow. You are spending a ton of time now in the gym, better known as "The Iron Church." As an aside, it makes me feel so close to you, Wells, as I did the exact same thing at the exact same time in my life! Back to the point though, when lifting, we systematically work on different muscles groups in order to force growth and increase capacity. The more pain we struggle through, the greater our strength. More reps equals more power.

It's exactly the same thing in terms of growing confidence. The more challenges we undertake, the more we stretch ourselves, the more we test our own abilities, the greater our personal power. Confidence builds greater confidence. Potential becomes virtually unlimited.

I want to close with something that is extremely important, son. You need to understand that the amazing trait of "self-confidence" has nothing to do with self. Confidence is a gift of God. Back to

Isaiah chapter 30 for a moment, the prophet reveals one of the single most remarkable truths within the entire history and experience of humanity. The statement is often overlooked which is almost impossible for me to understand because it is an absolute game changer for all of us who are paying attention. Isaiah tells us simply that the Lord longs to be gracious to us. Make sure you get that. The God of the universe *"longs to be gracious to you."* He wants you to be all you can be; he desires to bless you, and he is personally interested in your achievements.

With increasing and growing confidence, there is nothing outside of your grasp. Get after it, Wells. No limits.

Love you so much,
Dad

The
Thirty-Fifth Letter

Learnings

Dear Wells,

Demonstrations are not uncommon to see in Chicago. There are issues that people feel strongly about and the resulting rallies and gatherings frequently clog the sidewalks and streets downtown. These types of things are generally ignored by business people going about their daily regimens, but occasionally we need to wade through them in order to get to a destination. This happened last week for me. As I worked my way through the crowd, I got a great sense for the people who were part of this particular group and had a chance for a few minutes to really observe them. To be honest, I was rather disappointed.

Before I share my observations, I want to tell you that the freedom we have as Americans to voice our opinions is an amazing thing. We live in one of the most remarkable countries on earth, and I am deeply grateful for the freedoms that we enjoy including the right to gather and to express ourselves. Dissent is a powerful part of a self-governing republic, and the founders of our country (especially Thomas Jefferson) were keen to embrace it. The people of our nation should always possess a much greater power than our government. In other words, the crowd that I cut through had every right and privilege to be there. I am unsure however that many of them actually knew why they were there.

As I bumped through the pack, I was immediately aware that only about one quarter of the crowd actually seemed interested in what they were doing. Many of the people were engaged in random conversations or absent-mindedly texting. Others appeared to be sightseeing and taking pictures. Some seemed simply bored. The appearance of the people also was interesting. In general, the participants were young males dressed in a haphazard array of clothing bordering on slovenly. There were clearly some homeless people mixed in as well, and the entire gaggle was rambling along with no semblance of order. Rather than casting judgment, let's see what we can learn.

Wells, I believe that people need a purpose. There has to be a reason to do what we do. We have talked often about the importance of having goals and striving for an objective or outcome. The process of working for something keeps you focused and moving forward in your life. It forces you to make good decisions, and it gives you context and structure. It reminds you to use time wisely and not waste it. I am not sure that many of those people I saw on the street in Chicago had a purpose in their protestation efforts, maybe they just wanted to be part of the crowd.

Secondly, appearance is important. If you want people to take you seriously, it's imperative to dress well, possess solid social skills, and appear decent. Your look does not have to be expensive but one that demonstrates that you made an effort to be groomed and clean—it is a sign of self-respect and inspires respect from others. Your speech should be grammatically correct. For better or worse, stereotypes exist in our society, and people will judge you immediately based on your appearance. Part of the reason that the group in Chicago was ignored was simply their "look." So be mindful of what you are projecting.

Finally, if you want to do something or change something, be disciplined, intentional, and thoughtful about it. I am very proud of you in this regard simply because I see you doing this now in the way you are changing your body with strength training. You have a plan, you sought guidance and expertise around the "how," and you are systematically following a regimen over time. The results are awesome! This type of approach is what is needed to lead any type of change. The crowd in Chicago accomplished nothing more than wasting time. There was no plan, no regimen, no follow-up, and no discipline.

I am finishing this letter to you coming back from a quick trip to New York. You and Claire just arrived home for the holidays, and I will see you in a few hours. I can't wait!

Love you tons!
Dad

The
Thirty-Sixth Letter

God's Desires

Dear Wells,

We just finished a beautiful Christmas season together as a family. It is so wonderful to have you and your sister home from college. I love you both so much and having us all together is one of my greatest joys. The Christmas church service was also surprisingly good with a great sermon, beautiful music, and gorgeous decorations. While the retelling of the Christmas story is ever present and always welcome, it was one of the ancillary readings that really caught my attention this year.

The second reading at church on Christmas Day was from the first chapter of Hebrews. For the most part, this particular letter from the Bible is like reading an engineering textbook. It was written for a group of people who regarded extensive rules and requirements as critical to spirituality. The Jewish faithful of the time were highly educated and incredibly well versed in their knowledge of the Torah, Hebrew law, and of the history of their ancestors. As such, approaching them required research, context, and thoroughness. The Book of Hebrews has all of these things in spades.

In the first chapter, the author sets the table for the birth of the Messiah by referencing writings from the prophets. What is interesting and missed typically by a casual listener is simply that the references are not overt quotations nor are they directly credited. In other words, unless you knew the writings of the prophets of old (and the Jewish people did), you would assume that the ideas and words were original.

Here it is, "For to which of the angels did he ever say, 'Thou art my son, today I have begotten thee?'" That verse is Hebrews chapter 1, verse 5.

Now compare it to this, "Thou art my Son. This day I have begotten Thee. Ask of Me and I will give you the nations for thine inheritance and the uttermost regions of the earth for Thy possessions." That is from Psalm 2, written by David over one thousand years before Christ was born.

Wells, David wrote these words not only to foretell the coming of the Messiah. He wrote them for you and me and for all who believe. We've talked before about how God "longs to be gracious to us." We are his children. He desires great outcomes for us just as much as we want them for ourselves.

Almost every day, I pray these words from Hebrews and from David. I am so grateful that I am God's son, and I am grateful that he hears me when I pray. Always remember the words of Jesus on prayer, "Whatsoever you ask when you pray, believe that you have received it, and it will be yours." This is one of God's greatest promises to us, and it should fill you with hope. You see, son, you can have anything in life that you want. You just have to believe and have faith.

Sitting in that pew in church at Christmas and thinking through the import of these words also reminded me of another important truth. Simply this—there is frequently huge value and opportunity outside of the main event. For example, I am willing to bet that most of the people in that church were focused totally on the story of Christ's birth and completely missed the words from Hebrews and David. We have to always be vigilant for learnings and experiences that come to us when we least expect them. Sometimes the unexpected side dish tastes better that the main course.

Love you so much, son, and I am very proud of you.
Dad

The
Thirty-Seventh Letter

New Year's Day

Dear Wells,

On this past New Year's Day, Claire and I got up early and headed to the gym. The roads were quiet on a bright winter morning. The revelry from the night before probably had most people still in their beds. We felt great and were excited to get a workout in to start the New Year. To be truthful, it was also just plain fun to be together with the world still asleep around us. We pulled into the near empty parking lot at around 7:30 a.m., and we were just in time to see a new Bentley Turbo R pulling out.

It took a few minutes for us to process it, but we took quite a bit away from what we saw that morning. I am not focusing at all on the Bentley, though it is truly a magnificent car. It was gleaming, beautiful, and incredibly expensive. Those cars are hand made with workmanship and detailing that is very rare in the automotive world. What intrigued us about the Bentley was the probable nature and will of the person who was driving it.

You see, Wells, we felt pretty good about our level of effort when we headed out to the gym shortly after 7:00 a.m. on that New Year's Day morning. We realized when that Bentley pulled out of the parking lot that the guy driving it had already worked out, showered, and was on the road to his next thing. He was way ahead of us. The conclusion we came to was fairly clear: if you want a car like that or frankly anything special in this life, you have to be willing to outwork everyone else. Claire and I talked about this for a while that morning and painted a picture of the driver of that car. We figured that he was driven to succeed, goal oriented, disciplined, and relentless. He wanted something and then went after it.

The point of this letter is not to discuss some guy in a Bentley but rather to explore the way in which God fulfills promises. I wrote to you recently and shared my thoughts around a few verses from the Bible that hold incredible promises for us. God essentially will give us whatever we ask. Here's the important part though—most of the time, it will require our blood, sweat, and tears to obtain what we want. We can have anything we want, but we have to work for it.

You remember the story from Exodus. God selected Moses to lead the Israelites out of their Egyptian captivity and promised to lead them to a land "flowing with milk and honey". After forty years of wandering in the desert, the Israelites arrived at the Promised Land only to find that it was densely populated with powerful nations and clans who were dead set on defending it. What a shock that must have been. After forty years of toughing it in the desert, they found out that the serious work had not yet even begun.

I believe that God wraps up his gifts to us in hardship and pain because it makes us better and stronger people. If wishes instantly came true without effort or sacrifice, humanity would likely be extinct by now. A study of the lives of people who win the lottery will prove out my theory. In most cases, unearned riches typically lead to ruined lives and tragedy.

So the next time you are frustrated with the amount of effort it is taking to make progress toward your goals or feel that you have reached the limits of your endurance, push yourself further. God promises that you will get what you want and will bless you richly through the process of getting there.

Love you so much, my only son!
Dad

The
Thirty-Eighth Letter

House Guests

Dear Wells,

As you know, for the past nine weeks, we have had a family living with us.

Their situation is very difficult, and your mother and I decided to offer them shelter for a few months while they got things headed in the right direction. The decision was challenging. On one hand, we felt compelled to be the arms of God here on earth by helping the helpless. However, I was also mindful of my primary role as a father, provider, and protector of you, your mom, and your sisters. I never want anything to jeopardize our family and the environment that we have built over the years. We prayed intensely about it, and in the end, we were led to have them with us. The experience has been an interesting one, and I thought I would share with you a few learnings from it since you are away at college now and sheltered from direct involvement.

As I reflect upon it, I've come to realize a few things about myself and gained a unique (and close-up) perspective into the intimate details of another family's life. The experience has been enriching, although at times both difficult and challenging. I will spare you the details of the day-to-day but instead offer a few of my thoughts as we traverse the weeks and months with this family.

The first thing that I recognize through this is simply that our family is very, very blessed. I know that we talk often about this together, and I also know that you are deeply aware of it. It's just that for the first time, we have been put side-by-side with a family with children of the same age. This comparative yardstick makes me keenly aware of God's beneficence to us and reminds me that we need to be seeking always for opportunities to give back. Remember the words of Jesus, "To whom much is given, much is expected?" I am so proud of the way you are using the gifts that God has given you, son. Your chosen path to pursue an engineering degree is impressive as is the great work ethic you have shown this year at college. It is wonderful to see you using your mind and talents, and it saddens me when I think of others who appear to let their gifts go to waste.

Secondly, it is clearer to me now more than ever that we must use our time wisely. Countless hours spent in front of the television or in other mindless pursuits are ones that you will never ever get back. We all need some rest and relaxation, but if you let these things run away with you, the results will be devastating. The cost in terms of lost opportunity and lack of personal growth is off the charts. Wasting time like this is literally a life stealer.

Thirdly, this experience reminds me of the importance of perspective in terms of how we react and respond to events that happen in our lives. As an example, let's say that a similar and challenging circumstance happens in the lives of two different people, I can promise you that these people will likely respond in very distinct fashions. One person may be derailed permanently, allowing their life to be disrupted and a negative attitude to dominate their thinking, sometimes even adopting a victim mentality. Another person might learn from the challenge, shift gears, and become sharper because of the experience. They may take control of their circumstances and commit to never being dependent on another. How do you respond when life deals you a knockdown or throws a challenge at you?

Finally, and this has been a tough one for me, I have finally recognized that the old expression of leading a horse to water but being unable to make it drink is absolutely true. You know that your dad is somewhat of a control freak, and I live with the strong impulse to move people and things toward constructive outcomes. I know now that you can do that for circumstances and things but you cannot do it with people. This is incredibly frustrating especially when you are witness to self-inflicted destructive behavior. At the end of the day, I now believe that we are called to pray for people, live our lives with purpose, and provide a solid example to those who are observing us. After that, the impact we have is totally in God's hands.

Keep doing what you are doing, Wells!

Love you so much!
Dad

The
Thirty-Ninth Letter

The Grind

Dear Wells,

We miss you so much around here. We miss your smile, your laugh, and your awesome sense of humor. Above all though, we just miss sharing life with you. The daily experiences that appear mundane on the surface are the fabric of life and family, and as we process them over dinner most evenings, I find myself wishing that you and Claire were right there with us. Summer is almost here though, and we are so excited that you will be coming home! These letters to you are no substitute for your presence, but I hope that when you read them, you think of us and know how much we miss you and love you.

As you know, your little sister, Emma, is progressing rapidly on the squash court. There is a huge disparity in the physical development and strength of the kids in her age group, and we frequently see her matched up against girls who are much bigger, stronger, and faster. She shoulders on though and her discouragement tends to be brief when things do not go her way. I am hopeful that her takeaways from the game of squash extend far beyond the physical. It is clear that she will gain strength, ability, and maybe even a ticket to college through her efforts, but I am seeing now that this game could hugely benefit her character.

The squash community is small, and these girls tend to play each other a fair amount as they age. This creates a certain tension among them as they become friendly off the court and competitive and nervous when they are forced to play each other. Emma faced off against one of these girls recently in a match to decide the consolation winner for a gold level tournament. Each of the girls had played each other before; they had practiced together, and they knew each other's style of play, strengths, and weaknesses. As I settled in to watch the best of a five game match and coach your sister, I had a feeling that this would be a challenge.

Emma started strong and with good form and confidence. She controlled the first game well and won it with a small margin. Her opponent committed a few costly errors that your sister was able to capitalize on and stay out in front. During the break, Emma seemed relaxed, confident, and focused on getting things done.

The second game was different. Her opponent tightened up and played flawlessly, gaining confidence with every point. She was chasing down everything too and frustrating Emma with her ability to stave off point winning shots. The match leveled at one game apiece, and I could feel Emma's creeping anxiety as she came off the court for water.

Game three was more of the same. When Emma came off the court now down two games to one, she was very upset and trying hard to check her emotions. Her breathing was ragged, and her eyes were tearing up. I coached her, got her head straight and sent her back on the court where she came away with a very narrow win to force the match into a deciding fifth game. As I suspected would happen, she won the final game handily to seal the victory and thoroughly disappoint her opponent.

I have been fascinated by this match and have been replaying it in my mind over the last few weeks. Not because of the squash but because of the things that we all can learn from it.

When people start a task or go after a goal, they usually have great intentions and belief in their ability to succeed. They also sometimes have some early success that bolsters their enthusiasm and confidence. The problem happens when the headwinds kick in and they begin to face adversity. Mike Tyson, the former world heavyweight boxing champion summed it up in his famous quip, "Everyone has a plan until they get punched in the mouth."

I was really proud of Emma in the way that she set her teeth, dug in, and refused to let this girl get the best of her on the court. I think that the way she overcame adversity that day gave her a long lasting confidence in herself that she will be able to draw from for years to come. The lesson for all of us is to do what Emma did and refuse to let hardship and adversity get the best of us.

The other thing that struck me was the fact that people all want to get through things easily and with as little effort as possible. Emma came off the court after winning that first game thinking that the match would be a walk in the park. Not so fast.

We need to understand that things worth having are typically fought for and not handed to us. In other words, we have to grind them out—just like Emma did in that exhausting five-game match.

There you have it, my son! Welcome the grind and the adversity knowing that it will build your character and get you ever closer to what you want.

Love you tons, and I'll see you in a few weeks!
Dad

The Fortieth Letter

Eye on the Prize

Dear Wells,

I am writing this to you from the middle of Lake Michigan. We are delivering the racing sailboat, Renegade, from its winter home in Holland, Michigan, over to Chicago. The weather today is interesting with solid rain, confused waves, and about seventeen knots of breeze from the north. It's a big body of water, and even in late May, water temps out here are barely forty degrees. It is never a trip to take for granted.

I've just come below deck for a rest, and as I sit with my laptop open thinking of you, I need to tell you how excited I am that you and Claire will be home from college in just a few days! Your mother and I talk incessantly about it, and we are both looking forward to having our arms around you soon. I know too that your engineering curriculum this freshman year has been tough academically, and you probably are more than ready for a break.

My work has been very busy of late with the hiring of a new team member and an extraordinary number of client meetings. I am hugely grateful for both of these things and can't help but reflect upon how these last three years have gone since I have switched roles at my firm. The blessings have been immeasurable, and I see massive possibilities on the horizon. Our team will likely expand further before the end of the year; we are considering several new opportunities; revenue trends are very favorable, and our client satisfaction is very high. The challenges have been great, but the victories have been greater.

You may not remember this, Wells, but I do, when we sat together as a family a bit over three years ago and discussed the change I was contemplating, the risk for the family, and the challenges that were on the table, you looked me in the eye and recommended that I move forward with it. You simply stated that you trusted me and that I "was good at stuff." You were only half kidding when you said it, but I knew in my heart that you believed in me and that you did not doubt my resolve and skills. I am grateful to you for your confidence in me, and I am here to tell you that I have that same confidence in you.

Nothing moves in a straight line, and for my business, the last few years have been filled with peaks and valleys, successes and failures, setbacks and comebacks. There have been sleepless nights and euphoric days, but as I reflect back on all of it, I recognize clearly that the path to the top of anything is certain to be a hard and rocky trail.

As you end your first year, remember that you have chosen a path that is hard. Electrical and computer engineering are difficult studies, and you need to know that your mother and I are hugely proud of you for taking the road less traveled. Today I want to encourage you. I want you to remember that nothing worthwhile comes without effort and pain. You know very well that the important thing is simply to always be moving forward—keeping your eye on your goal. Focus on seeing yourself wearing those graduation robes and holding that engineering degree firmly in your hand.

This boat is getting beat up a bit today as we fight through the fortieth mile of our trip. I am here to tell you that we will arrive at our goal. It may take a bit longer than we expected, we may have a few anxious moments on the way, but we will tie up in Chicago and get everything squared away perfectly in the end. The same was true for my business, and the same thing will hold true for your experience at college.

I am needed now on deck, so I will close by telling you the same thing that you told me a few years back. I believe in you, son. You are good at stuff!

Love you so much!
Dad

The Forty-First Letter

Three Keys

Dear Wells,

I just attended a meeting in New York with my company's chief executive officer and other members of the leadership team. The meeting itself was only moderately interesting, but in typical corporate fashion, our logo was emblazoned everywhere. After twenty-two years with the firm, I know the logo by heart, and it is embedded in my mind's eye. The three keys that comprise the graphic—each stand for one of the company's core principles. I won't bore you with the explanation, but I will tell you that as I get older, I have come to believe that there are also only three real keys to being happy and successful in this life. You will find that plenty of people will come at you with various recipes and ideas "guaranteed" to produce happiness and success, and you need to be wary. Most of this stuff may give you a temporary boost, but in the end, will always leave you disappointed. At the end of the day, that logo reminded me once again that if you cling to these three tenets, they will surely give you lasting joy, success, and peace.

The first key will likely surprise you coming from me—relationships. I have never been a loner, but I have historically placed a much higher emphasis on my family than I have on building friendships and deep relationships with other people. Over the last five years or so, I have realized though how important relationships are in our lives. God created us as social beings and the amount of energy, joy, and fulfillment that we can get through healthy interactions with others has surprised me. If I think about it further, I recognize that we are created in God's image and likeness, and if he desires our attention and love, it is not at all surprising to discover that we are built also to thrive on attention and love as well. A few final things here—make sure that your relationship with God is always first and is always strong. Talk to him daily and share your feelings and cares with him. He breathed life into you and "longs to be gracious to you." Secondly, be a giver in your relationships with others; this is not just about being generous materially but with attention and friendship. You will find that the paradox of giving is rewarding beyond description. Be discerning with whom you build relationships. Make sure the people who surround you build you up and propel you forward.

The second key in my view is to always be actively pursuing something. We talk all the time in our family about dreams and goals and many of my letters to you over the years touch on this theme. The fact is that it really doesn't matter what your goals are, it just matters that you are actively working toward them. That being said, I would encourage you to have big goals and big dreams. I am a firm believer that whatever we set our sights on, we can accomplish. Remember me telling you that God wouldn't have given us a vision for something unless he also gave us the tools to obtain it. So don't think small! The active pursuit of a goal gives you purpose and passion, wards off stagnation, and leaves little time for worry or fear.

The final key for me (and this one will come as no surprise to you) is physical health and fitness. Paul said in his letter to the Corinthians that our bodies are temples of the Holy Spirit, and by definition, we ought to respect that. Being fit makes you feel great physically and also makes you feel great about yourself. Self-confidence, mental prowess, energy level, attitude, and outlook all stem from your physical health. It's a foundation that you cannot overlook, so hit the gym hard and often and make sure you eat good food. A little cardio training with all those weights would go a long way too, son!

So there you have it, very simple and very powerful. Your mom and I pray for you every day, Wells. We want you to be sincerely happy and richly blessed in your life. Start with these three things and you will be well on your way.

Love you so much!
Dad

The
Forty-Second Letter

Going to Church

Dear Wells.

We had a great talk this morning, and I was so glad that you brought up your feelings about going to church. You said that it sometimes feels like you are just going in order to "check the box." While I think I had the right response, it's too important a topic to leave be after just a few minutes of conversation. I know you were in a hurry to hook up with your friends and get down to the music festival and that may have colored your thinking today. The fact is that I can't get it off my mind, so I thought I would spend a few hours this afternoon passing along my thoughts to you.

I totally understand your feelings by the way. On the surface, church services can be dry, lack good content, and be inconveniently timed for our schedules. If we just think about those things, we are bound to get frustrated and question why we even bother to go. The challenge for us all is to go beyond the surface and explore the hidden power and blessings that lay in store for those who are faithful and make going to church a must in their week.

You know me, I can't help but look into the book of Isaiah for guidance around this. He said in chapter 30, verse 15, "In repentance and rest is your salvation, in quietness and trust is your strength..."

This is a huge statement. Our lives are so busy, son. They wiz by filled with work, friends, events, and demands. If we don't take time to stop and reflect, we can lose our connection with the One who created us and lose touch with his blessings in our lives. That time in church on Sundays allows us to practice the words that Isaiah lays out and find rest, forgiveness, quietness, and trust. That time is meant to renew us and strengthen us.

The key, of course, is our own attitudes. I withheld the second part of the verse from Isaiah. The whole thing goes like this, "In repentance and rest is your salvation, in quietness and trust is your strength, but you would have none of it." You see, Wells, if we carry the wrong attitude around church on Sunday, we are forsaking the gifts that we can receive. We need to go with an open mind and a grateful spirit—intentionally looking for the blessings that God wants to bestow.

There's more. Later on in the book of Isaiah, the old prophet gets more specific around the gifts that we can receive from honoring God on Sundays and seeking him. This is from Chapter 58:

> If you call the Sabbath a delight and the Lord's holy day honorable, and if you honor it by not going your own way and not doing as you please or speaking idle words, then you will find your joy in the Lord, and I will cause you to ride in triumph on the heights of the land and to feast on the inheritance of your father Jacob.

It is interesting for me to note that even thousands of years ago people were the same. They were distracted by their "stuff" and always thinking about their own agendas on Sundays. The temptation to skip out on church and justify it was the same back then as it is now. Fight that tendency. Adjust your attitude and thinking on Sundays and make it to church with a thankful and open spirit. Enter through those doors seeking God's blessings and guidance in your life. Give him that time. As Isaiah says, "you will find your joy in the Lord" and "ride in triumph on the heights of the land."

Remember, it matters not who is giving the sermon or what the readings are. The only things that matter are your presence and God's.

Love you so much!
Dad

The
Forty-Third Letter

YOLO

Dear Wells,

We are starting to get acclimated to our new home and neighborhood. It has been about a month since we made the move, and I have to admit that it has been harder than we anticipated. Our family has never lived in the city before, and when you combine that with the fact that we downsized fairly significantly, the adjustment has been stressful. There have been a few times in the past weeks when your mom and I have looked at each other and wondered what we were thinking. We left a beautiful home in a great neighborhood with friends and comforts at every side and made a massive change for really no reason. There is still a long road ahead with renovations and decorating, taking things off to storage and simply feeling like our new place is home.

The overused expression YOLO (You Only Live Once) is usually thrown out there as an excuse to spend too much money, take too much risk, or to defend a goofy stunt. What is interesting to me is that the truth in those four words is often lost amidst the laughs. The reality is that life is fleeting and should be lived to its fullest. God has given us a very brief time here on earth, and I believe he desires us to enjoy the rich tapestry that is his creation.

I think you know that our family has been incredibly blessed with health, love, security, and other gifts. Along with all this, we have had the ability to accumulate many of the things that make our life comfortable. Beyond the essentials, these things are typically just icing on the cake. They may satisfy a temporary craving but rarely give us any lasting joy or satisfaction. The journey that leads us to the attainment of things frequently provides more value than does the actual ownership. In other words, if you set a goal to own a particular thing and then work hard toward it, the development of your strength and character in the process is far more valuable to you in your life than the resulting achievement of your goal. I guess what I am trying to say is that the experiences you collect in your life are far more important than the things you actually possess.

We chose to leave our comfortable situation in the suburbs because we wanted to sample a new experience. We wanted to feel the vibrancy of the city, see the diversity of life, and put ourselves in the pathway of something new. It was absolutely the right decision, and we are loving it. This is an example of my belief that change is always a good thing in our lives.

I read recently the account of Jesus recruiting his disciples. In Matthew chapter 4, we see that Jesus was walking on the beach and comes across the fishermen, Peter, and his brother, Andrew. He says to them, "come and follow me," and the scripture says that they at once left their nets and followed. The same thing happens with James and John just a few verses later. What we don't read about here is the fact that these men had been fishermen their entire lives. They were born into it; it was all they knew, and they had been doing it longer then they could remember. All of a sudden, they dropped everything and made a frightening and dramatic change. It was so monumental that likely no one in their village, community, or family had ever heard of anything like it ever happening before. It was probably an event that was talked about for years.

You know the end of the story—these men went on to become history and world changers simply because they were willing to make a definitive and voluntary shift.

So my son, I want you to always be open to change. I hope that you will consistently seek out new experiences and horizons. Never let yourself get stale—who knows, you may also change the world.

Love you so much!
Dad

The
Forty-Fourth Letter

Putting Others First

Dear Emma and Wells,

I have been waiting for this moment for a long time! It is the first time that I am addressing a letter to the two of you! Your thirteenth birthday this week, little one, makes it the perfect opportunity for me to start including you in the monthly letters that I send out to your brother. From this point forward, expect something from me every month until you turn twenty. I know that we talk all of the time, but sometimes there are things that I want to say that are too important to gloss over or be lost in a random conversation. Our family is everything to me, and I love you all more than you can possibly know. I am so grateful that God has appointed me as your father, and I pray daily that he would grant me the wisdom and strength that I need.

It has been a huge joy for me to watch the two of you grow up together. You have always had a very special love for each other, and it is something that I hope and pray will never be lost. You treat each other with a love and respect that is unfortunately not that common anymore even within families. The challenge for all of us is to extend that same love and respect to everyone that we meet.

We all have some natural tendencies as human beings that sometimes don't serve us very well in today's world. They likely stem from our past when simply surviving from day to day was a difficult challenge. Selfishness, defensiveness, and isolationism are just a few of these tendencies that if left unchecked can create an unhappy and incomplete life.

Try always to think of the needs of others before your own. While this may sound a bit strange, you will find that when you meet the needs of others, your needs will be met all the more quickly. The principle is similar to the phrase that "giving is better than receiving." The mental and psychological rewards that stem from unselfish behavior are too numerous to list but include peace, happiness, and joy. You will also find that the more you act unselfishly, the more people will be attracted to you.

Be quick to forgive and to also accept responsibility. Defensive behavior can often lead us to point fingers at others or at situations to explain away our shortcomings. This is a sure way to never be all that we are destined to be. Acting like this can teach us to hold onto grudges or to always be looking for excuses. Wells and Emma, your destiny is on your shoulders—you have control. Make sure that you set the right course.

Build relationships and grow them. Seek friends, connections, and common interests with people. God has breathed his Spirit into each one of us, and we derive huge benefits from our interactions with others. That being said, make sure that the people you seek out and bring close to you are the ones that can build you up and the ones that you can build into. The older I get, the more I recognize the immense power of positive nurturing relationships. There are huge rewards for you in every aspect of your life by getting out there in the community and breaking out of your shell. Remember always the words of Jesus, "Seek and you shall find, knock and the door will be open for you." This is true for all things both positive and negative. Make sure that you are seeking good things, good people, and good goals.

So my thought for you as we wrap up our Thanksgiving week together is simply to take that love, respect, and patience that you have for each other and extend it out. Show it to others with consistency, and I promise that you will be awestruck by the results.

Love you both so much!
Dad

The
Forty-Fifth Letter

Overflow

Dear Wells and Emma,

A few weeks ago in church, one of the readings recounted the miracle of the five loaves and two fishes. You remember the story—Jesus was teaching out in the wilderness and after a long day, he recognized that the crowd (some five thousand men along with additional women and children) was getting famished. There was nowhere to go, no food vendors around, and it was probably getting dark. The apostles saw no way out, but Jesus instructed them to find out what food was available. They came back with a report that they had found five loaves and two fishes and of course told Jesus that it clearly wouldn't be of any use. After all, what good is so little amongst so many?

God did what God does. Jesus blessed the food and had his people pass it around. The five thousand plus was fed and completely satisfied and then more than twelve basketfuls of left overs were picked up. The danger of hearing this story so much is that we tend to get a bit jaded by it. It seems like it's another miracle in a string of miracles performed by Jesus, and we have been hearing it since we could barely walk. I want you to focus on it for a minute—right here and right now. There are a few things going on that are unbelievably important, and if you recognize them, they will give you a life changing confidence and assurance.

First, the God of the universe who created the heavens and the earth is absolutely concerned with your well-being and comfort. Think about it, Jesus recognized that the people who had been listening to him and following him had a minor physical need: they were hungry, and he took care of it. Most people go through their lives and either never call out to God or do so only in the event of a crisis. Emma and Wells, God cares for you so much that he looks to satisfy even your slightest discomfort if you will let him. As Isaiah says, "We are like a polished arrow in his quiver," we are "fearfully and wonderfully made," and he "covers us with the palm of his hand." Remember this always and pray for his care every day. Nothing is too small for his attention.

The second thing that strikes me about the miracle of the loaves and fish is the fact that the disciples had to pick up twelve baskets of leftovers from the crowd. The entire crowd ate until they were satisfied, and there was still plenty of extra food. In other words, there was more than enough for everyone. This tells me that God not only wants to meet our needs but he wants to give us abundance. He desires that there is more than enough for us and constantly tells us (in word and deed) that our cup will overflow. You must believe this. Whenever you feel yourself thinking about scarcity or lack, remember the miracle of the loaves and fishes.

Along these lines also, always celebrate another person's success. As human beings, we have a tendency to feel jealous or competitive when someone achieves greatness or celebrates a big accomplishment. Don't. This type of thinking comes from the assumption that success and achievement are limited resources and that the accomplishment of someone else will somehow take away from your opportunity. Not so. Remember, God provides abundance; there is more than enough. You will have as much success and achievement in your life as you desire.

Finally, my children, always be on the lookout for his favor and love. He changed water into wine at a wedding in Cana just because he knew it would give people joy. Remember that God will bless you just because you are precious to him. Leave your bedroom every morning with an expectant heart and faith-filled spirit.

Love you both!
Dad

The
Forty-Sixth Letter

Pain and Growth

Dear Wells and Emma,

What is it that makes someone great? What is it that makes them stand out in the world and lead lives that are different? Why do some people stand on podiums, receive awards, and become the subject of books and newspaper headlines? The more important question is probably the how. How do these people do what they do?

I am just now finishing a great book by David Shenk. His book, *The Genius in All of Us*, goes a long way to dispelling the common myth that talents are something we are born with versus something that we develop. It is easier to believe that someone is born with skills because that takes the pressure off of us. It gives us an easy excuse. I believe that if you want to be really good at something, it takes a mix of natural ability, persistence, desire, determination, and work. I remember, Wells, when you were very young what amazing balance you had. The first time you got on a bike (I think you were only three), you just took off. It took quite a bit of hard work, persistence, and determination for you to master the unicycle and become so amazing on the skateboard though!

Emma, you are an incredibly talented squash player with a great work ethic and a strong desire to be at the very top of your sport. The competitive streak that resides in you is very much like my own and can produce disappointment and pain in defeat and incredible joy in victory. This last weekend at the tournament in Delaware, you felt that awful pain. Losing those two matches in front of family, friends, and former coaches was hard, especially knowing that your ability was there but somehow inaccessible. How you respond to situations will likely define you. In fact, it is this type of situation that defines us all.

Everyone comes across forks in the road during their lives, and I believe this may be just one of those moments in your life, Emma. After going through something like you did, some people decide that all the effort and pain are just not worth it. They decide that the road is too hard, the goal is too far away, and the sacrifices that must be made to achieve come at too high a cost. In other words, they give up on their dream and take the easy road. More rarely, however, a person goes through defeat, pain, and discouragement and comes out the other side with more strength, more determination, and more tools that will ultimately make that person into something really special.

I recently read through the book of Daniel again and thought about those three teenagers who stubbornly refused to compromise. Shadrach, Meshach, and Abednego had amazing willpower, discipline, and courage. As an aside, it is pretty clear that they were athletes themselves. They ate a strict diet and were described as incredibly healthy. To make a long story short, they refused to back off of their beliefs even in the face of being burned alive. The king got so angry that he had the furnace heated to such a level that it killed the workers who were responsible for throwing in the bound-up teens. After these three boys were thrown in, they walked through absolutely unharmed. Here's the part I want you to focus on though—*the only thing that got burned off of them were the ropes that were being used to bind them up.*

Have that same belief and faith. When you go through pain, setbacks, discouragement, and the feeling that you are being thrown into the fire, know that the process is making you stronger, increasing your resolve, furthering your path toward greatness, and burning off things that are holding you back.

Love you both so much!
Dad

The
Forty-Seventh Letter

Mastering Emotions

Dear Emma and Wells,

I heard recently that people make all of their decisions in life based on their emotions. After the decision is made, they may rationalize it or justify it through reasoning and intellect but the actual decision is made only with their feelings.

Our feelings are an unbelievable gift from God. The joy, love, happiness, peace, and excitement that we get to experience are an incredible part of being human. Our emotions are truly an amazing piece of our lives, and it's impossible to think of being without them. The challenge though is to make sure that your feelings are serving you instead of you serving your feelings. A life led by emotion will be a disappointing one at best and can even turn tragic if left unchecked.

Your dad worked closely a few years ago with a man who had expensive tastes and zero self-control. On the surface, it looked like he had it made. Beautiful cars, expensive watches, designer clothes— he bought anything he wanted. People who did not know him well would envy him because of all his possessions. As time unfolded, I learned quite a bit from him. The first takeaway was a stark reminder that money and possessions have nothing to do with happiness. In fact, I have come to believe that they sometimes have the opposite effect. As I watched this guy accumulate all his stuff, it was obvious that he was trying unconsciously to satisfy some need in his life. Owning all of these beautiful things was clearly not making him fulfilled, yet he kept going with it. After a while, it became evident that the immense pile of shiny things had only served to destroy his peace along with his finances. Keep your own desire for "stuff" in check. It is fantastic to want a few nice things and to have a goal to achieve them, but make sure you are not letting your feelings and desires run things for you as my colleague did. It led him to financial ruin and deep depression.

I can also tell you from personal experience that decisions made in anger or in the heat of the moment are invariably wrong and will lead you down bad pathways. Remember when Peter denied that he knew Jesus? He did so with swearing and a hot temper. I bet that moment was the biggest regret of his life. Always be sure that your decisions are made with a level head, and don't be afraid to wait out your feelings if your blood pressure is running high.

Pride, jealousy, fear, and other emotions can also cause us to make foolish choices. It's amazing what humans are capable of when we let our emotions run our lives. Many of the most watched videos on the internet get that way because they are cataloguing people doing something incredibly stupid. Tragically also, history is full of people doing unspeakable things to one another simply because they let their emotions and feelings guide them. Cain killing Abel in a fit of jealousy way back at the beginning set the stage for innumerable troubles—all stemming from letting our feelings get the best of us.

For so many reasons, one of my favorite stories about Jesus was when the scribes and Pharisees brought a woman to him who was caught in the very act of adultery. They were so excited to entrap him as the law of the day was pretty clear. What's relevant here is that Jesus took his time in responding. If you remember, he was sitting down and drawing in the sand with his fingers while he collected his thoughts. Instead of snapping off a decision born of emotion, he came up with one of the single greatest responses in all of scripture.

So Emma and Wells, embrace your feelings! I pray every day that you would feel happiness, joy, gratitude, peace, and love. Remember though to be masters of your feelings and not servants of them.

Love you so much!
Dad

The
Forty-Eighth Letter

The Easter Dog

Dear Emma and Wells,

Easter Sunday this year was incredible. It was such a blessing to be together as a family. We don't see as much of one another now given college and school commitments, and I really cherish the time when we are with each other.

As we made our way toward Easter services at the cathedral in Los Angeles, I remembered walking with my arms around you and thanking God for bringing you both into my life. I entered that church with a heart full of gratitude and a joyful expectation of honoring God on that Sunday morning.

An enormous cross of lilies hung over the entrance, and we were all stuck by the sheer size of the building and the number of people present. We sat very near the front, and as the service unfolded with all its sights, sounds, and pageantry, I found myself drawn to something else entirely—something very simple and absolutely captivating. Despite the beauty of the church and the service, a young blind man riveted my attention. The man was handsome and strong looking but plainly dressed with dark glasses and simple attire. By his side sitting quietly was a beautiful black Labrador. Their appearances were in no way remarkable. What made the image so moving was the mutual love and dependence that radiated from them both. Their unique and special relationship became more apparent as the service progressed.

The dog would routinely look up to his master with a look of pure loyalty and love. It is hard to describe the emotion reflected in the dog's expression. You got the sense that the dog would have chosen no other life in the world but to care for, guide, and love that man. When the congregation sat, the dog would rest his head on the man's thigh. There was no expectation; it just seemed that the dog felt that perhaps it would be comforting for him to do so.

As for the blind man, he appeared physically strengthened by the dog's presence and proximity. Their constant contact with each other seemed to empower him in some way. He didn't look vulnerable but strong with life and vibrant. Occasionally, when they were sitting together with the dog's head resting on his thigh, the man would lean down and quietly press his face against the dog's. In those moments, you could feel the bond and love emanating from them both.

Many questions have been running through my mind since that Easter Sunday experience. Can God use a dog to bring love and joy to a life? Was this man's blindness somehow a blessing that introduced him to such love and joy? Do I take relationships with people who love me for granted? Should I allow myself to lean on those who love me? Do I show my love without regard for what people might think?

More questions come: What's important in life? Is it purpose? Is it relationship? Is it love?

Dear children, please reflect on these questions as I have, and be sure to look for the big things in the small. When you enter into a routine situation, let your heart be open in case there is something powerful to be seen. Look for the love around you, and never miss a message that God may be sending no matter what the messenger may look like—even if it's a dog.

Love you both so much!
Dad

The
Forty-Ninth Letter

The Paradox of Giving

Dear Wells and Emma,

I just applied to be a volunteer for the American Red Cross! A few weeks ago, I attended a breakfast in Chicago that highlighted some of the amazing people who have been involved with the Red Cross. They are all just normal folks going about their lives, and when called, they do extraordinary things. As the breakfast meeting unfolded, many of these volunteers received awards and recognition for their service. When they accepted, each one of them was extremely humble and talked about how it was a blessing to be able to serve.

Closer to home, your mom has been doing quite a bit of volunteer work recently over at the St. Vincent De Paul Center. It's been amazing to watch her become involved like this in our community. She is an unbelievable woman, and I thank God every day that he has put her into my life. What's really interesting about her volunteer work is that it is really invigorating her. As much as she is now a blessing to others, I cannot help but notice that the blessing in her own life is twice as rich. This is the paradox of giving. Perhaps St. Francis said it best when he pronounced that "it is in giving that we receive."

As recent weeks have gone by, I have been thinking more about this and recently read a study about the impact of volunteer service on one's happiness and fulfillment in life. It turns out that there is an absolute and measurable correlation. This particular study concluded that those who give more than 100 hours per year in volunteer effort are markedly and measurably happier and joy-filled.

There's more around this paradox of giving also. The Bible abounds with stories of those who become incredibly blessed because of their generosity. The concept works not only with time, like in volunteering, but also with money and other resources. You may remember the story of Elijah and a poor widow from the book of Kings. Elijah asked her for water in the midst of a drought, and she gave it to him. He asked her for food, and she gave him the very last thing that she had. She fully expected that she and her son would die of starvation and despite this gave away to a stranger all she had. The result was that her jar of flour and jug of oil never ran dry. Because of her generosity, she was blessed with unending abundance.

Is it possible that by giving more we actually receive more? Is this some kind of universal principle? Does it apply to all areas of our life? Money? Time? Love? If we give these things, do we receive a higher amount of them in return?

I am beginning to understand that the answer is yes.

The other thing to consider is the way we feel when we volunteer or give something away with no expectation of anything in return. Acts of kindness always produce more happiness and joy for the giver than they do for the receiver.

So, my children, I invite you to test this out for yourselves. I know you both are busy with school, friends, and interests, but I am wondering if there is a huge gift for you that is waiting dormant—ready for you to pick up and dust off.

Love you both so much!
Dad

The Fiftieth Letter

The Slight Edge

Dear Emma and Wells,

Every morning when I wake up, I spend time in prayer thanking God for the two of you and for your beautiful sister. Your Mom and I are incredibly proud and deeply grateful to have had a hand in starting you on life's great journey. Today when I awoke, I was a bit surprised by the speed of time. As I start this letter, it is June 13th my son, your 20th birthday.

I had always planned to cease sending these letters after you pass through your teenage years, and I will remain faithful to that. The discipline is challenging though—I feel that there is so much more that I want to tell you. For better or worse, I will always do so, though it will be in conversation rather than in writing.

Wells, I wanted to tell you again how much I loved our time together over breakfast at CBA a few weeks ago. It means the world to me when you seek out my guidance and advice. It is a joy to spend time with you, and I pray that my words would carry helping wisdom and guidance for you as you go through the challenges that form character.

I am reading a wonderful book right now by Jeff Olson called *The Slight Edge*. I would say that it is remarkable in how unremarkable it is. There is no giant breakthrough revealed, no magic bullet offered, no pearls of advice worth millions granted. It does, however, point out the central ingredient to success in life. Jeff calls it the "slight edge," but you and I know it better as a simple combination of self-discipline, time, and repeated positive actions. In other words, there are no shortcuts.

The thing is—that is good news! It means that anyone can accomplish anything they set their mind on and are willing to work for. It means, Wells, that you can get straight As, work for a cool tech firm, live in the mountains, and be profoundly happy. For you, Emma, it means that you can become one of the top junior squash players in the country and have colleges fighting over you. You both can be whoever and do whatever you want if you are willing to apply the daily disciplines and repeated positive actions over time.

As you get older, you will notice that most people don't come close to reaching their potential. It's not that they are bad people, it's just that they don't want to put in the effort or the time to be all that they can be. We all want things now, and we don't want to wait. We want to buy the winning lottery ticket, find the buried treasure, and hit the hole in one without having to work for it. This stuff only happens in the movies though, and you are probably realizing that things worth having are worth striving for each and every day.

I have more good news: the stuff that gets you to where you want to go isn't that hard to do. It is simply making a promise to do it and not slacking off. It's the intention of studying a certain amount of time every day. It's the commitment to stick to your guns and ignoring the temptations and people who will try and knock you off your path. Always remember though that the things that are easy to do are also easy not to do. An excuse here and there can really derail you!

So, my dear son, I guess this is it. Please know that I am always by your side, always in your corner, and always proud of you. T. Pain and Maino wrote a song that I like called "All the Above." In it, there is a simple and profound line that is meaningful in my life, and I pray that it would be powerful in yours as well.

Be on a mission to be who you were destined to be.

Love you so much! Godspeed!
Dad

The Fifty-First Letter

Scripture Power

Dear Emma,

I love the fact that you enjoy reading so much. There is no better way for you to expand your mind, explore new worlds, and broaden your horizons. Some books are much better than others, but today I want to share with you a bit about the most fascinating, exciting, and life changing book out there. I stumbled across it when I was your age and still can't believe how good it is. It is full of the most amazing things! Acts of courage, feats of daring, and roadmaps that will guarantee to take you wherever you want to go. It has adventure, terrifying villains, superhuman heroes, and the greatest love story ever told. The book that I am talking about, Emma, is the Bible.

There was a cool movie called *The Book of Eli* that came out in 2010. Critics panned the thing, and audiences for the most part yawned at it. The story followed the normal lines of good guys and bad guys, hardship and strife, pleasure and pain. None of this made the film stand out. What was truly unique was the fact that this movie focused squarely on the boundless and incredible power of the words contained within the Bible.

The movie follows a wanderer named Eli who in a devastated world with few people and no resources carries a Bible with him in a quest to find a proper home for it. There are very few books left in this world, and Carnegie, the central villain, searches relentlessly for a copy of the Holy Scriptures. With ruthless obsession, he kills, maims, and stops at absolutely nothing in order to get his hands on a copy. When asked by Eli why he wants the book, Carnegie replies:

> I grew up with it. I know its power. Imagine how righteous this world could be if we had the right words for our faith. People would truly understand why they are here and what they are doing.

Even though he wanted this Bible for his own selfish ambitions, Carnegie believed that the words of the Bible would enable people to have unlimited power and achieve unprecedented heights. He believed in the promises contained in the Bible and was convinced of its potency.

While the story line is fine and the film is good entertainment, I am here to tell you that *Carnegie was right*. The Bible contains words of promise and power that can alter the course of a person's destiny.

Amazingly enough—no one seems to know it. In today's world, most families could turn up a copy of the Bible without too much trouble. It has become overly familiar to us, and the Law of Familiarity says that over time, luster and enthusiasm for anything fades. The stories in the Bible have become trite and stale. Some scoff at them, some embrace, but most ignore. The news of the day or the latest and greatest show/app/game/tech/book catches our eye instead. We are like dogs chasing squirrels or bugs flying toward the brightest light in the neighborhood.

The result is simply that most people pay no attention to the Bible and subsequently are missing out on the single greatest gift to mankind. To be frank, the words of the Bible are perhaps the most significant source of power in our universe. They sit dormant on your iPhone.

Emma, don't miss out! Read this unbelievable book. Study it; think about it and let the words sink into you. I guarantee that it will change your life.

Love you so much!
Dad

PS: Let's kick around together what books in the Bible would be interesting for you to read right now!
XO

The
Fifty-Second Letter

Journaling

Dear Emma,

I started keeping a journal about a year ago and have made a commitment to write in it at least five days a week. Sometimes it is just a few lines, and other times, the passages are longer. As I get older, I am very aware that time is quickly going by, and I don't want to take a second of it for granted. I have found that if I open my journal at the end of the day with a pen in my hand, it reminds me to reflect on the events, people, and blessings that have just gone by. There is beauty in the ordinary, hidden gems in the mundane, and bits of wisdom that can change your life if you take time to think about them.

Our family lives such an amazing life. We are blessed beyond description and pack an incredible amount of activities into every day. Work, school, squash, activities, friends, travel, and dozens of other things make time whiz by. The danger is that we are mostly too busy to slow down and enjoy the rich tapestry of our lives or to even think about its deeper meaning.

A journal helps with all of that. When I write at the end of the day, I have a chance to pause and think about what happened in the preceding hours and live those experiences again. That alone is an opportunity. Good things get enjoyed for a second time, memories are made, and possibilities for learning can be processed without the heat or pain of the moment.

Socrates supposedly said that "an unexamined life is not worth living." It's hard to disagree with that. If we don't take time to really inspect ourselves, our thoughts, our growth, and our lessons, I would say that we are likely missing the point of life. I often think of Jesus and his constant habit of going off by himself to pray, reflect, and fast. I imagine that if it was easy back then to keep a journal, he definitely would have done so.

When I open up that journal every night, I always first read my entries from the past day or two. It makes me remember and relive again the happenings of the days gone by and almost always brings a smile to my face. I am so mindful of our blessings and am so grateful for what God has given us. The things that we get to do are truly remarkable, and it is a pleasure to live them more than once. Sometimes tough things are in there and going through them again, even if it is painful, reinforces the lesson.

The last sentence of every entry starts with the letters: WDILT, my own shorthand for "What Did I Learn Today." You know me by now, Emma. I am always looking to get better and improve myself. Taking the time to really think about the day and then combing through it is much like a prospector looking for a piece of gold. Sometimes it takes a while, but it is well worth it.

So, little one, how about you give it a try? If you would start this habit now, it might just impact your whole life for the better. Let's chat about it, and if you would like, I'll buy you a beautiful notebook of your choosing to get you started.

Love you so much!
Dad

The
Fifty-Third Letter

God's Love

Dear Emma,

Every night for a very long time, after the day was done and the books were read, your Mom and me would tuck you into bed, turn the lights off and pray over you. It was the way we ended our days, and it was a time that I truly miss. I will never forget pulling those covers up to your chin and kissing your beautiful hair.

I am sure you remember the prayers as well; we always started with the Lord's Prayer and ended with me saying the same thing. The words became grooved into my mind and heart over the years, and I am wondering if they have been grooved into yours. Do you remember? Before I left your bedside, I would always whisper, "Lord, I pray that Emma would come to know you at a young age and walk with you her whole life."

Dear one, that is my greatest wish for you still! And now with your confirmation into the church coming so soon around the corner, it is something that I hope you will really think about.

The love of our God for each of us is so beautiful, so sincere, so huge, and so selfless that it defies our ability to comprehend it. He craves our attention and wants nothing more than to shower us with his goodness and grace. You know how I am always hugging you

155

and wanting us to spend time together. Imagine that multiplied by a thousand!

It is so easy to lose touch with God's love though. I am convinced that it can only really be felt in the quiet, and those times are exceedingly rare these days unless we seek them out. Just this week, I was walking along the Chicago River on a beautiful day. Perfect sunshine and a delightful breeze caused my soul to lift; I started to just thank God for his incredible gifts. It was like he was there next to me, smiling and happy to simply be there with me. How often do we miss those moments? Look around you anytime during your day, and you will see that eight out of ten people are completely oblivious to the beauty around them. They are staring at their phones or blasting music through headphones. These are not bad things at all, but if they are constant in our lives, we might be missing out on God's greatest gift—the feeling of his love.

You know how I love to read the Book of Isaiah. The promises and insights in there are so incredible. Isaiah reveals a lot to us about not only God's love for us but also quite a bit about how God *views* us. He calls us a "crown of splendor," a "polished arrow in his quiver," and a "royal diadem" in his hand. That's amazing. Not only does he love us, but he also thinks we are incredible! He is proud of us and cherishes us.

So Emma, as you think about your confirmation, I hope and pray that you would be open to feeling God's love in your life and believe in yourself the way he believes in you! Seek him from time to time by reading his Word or focusing your energy and attention. Listen for him in the quiet times.

I will continue to pray like I always have, "Lord, I pray that Emma would come to know You at a young age and walk with You her whole life."

Love you so much, dear!
Dad

The
Fifty-Fourth Letter

Goals

Dear Emma,

We have talked so much, you and I, about goals and the importance of going after things that you want in life. It doesn't matter if the goal is success in school, admittance to a specific college, earning money to pay for something, or crossing the finish line in first place. You and I know that none of these things will get accomplished unless you set that objective and then work relentlessly toward its achievement. It takes effort, courage, persistence, pain, and most of the time tears to achieve anything worthwhile.

I have been fortunate to have hit many of the goals that I have set for myself over the years. It is hugely satisfying, but to be honest, the satisfaction is never permanent. The interesting thing about us as humans is that we always want more. That desire to constantly improve, seek, and yearn is a powerful force and one that drives us to new heights. For example, when you ran a mile in less than eight minutes, you immediately wanted to break seven minutes. When you became ranked in the top fifty squash players in the United States, you wanted to get into the top forty. My point is simply that it never stops.

That is a good thing. The wonderful thing about pursuing a goal is not in whether or not you achieve it, but rather the person that you become in going for it. When you really go after a goal, you apply self-discipline, you work really hard, you sharpen skills, and you push yourself mentally and physically past levels that you thought possible. In other words, the beauty is in the becoming.

We are who we are because of the road we travel. We are people of excellence because of the pain and effort that we have expended. Whether or not we achieve a goal is less important than the person we become when we are going for it.

You have probably heard by now about what typically happens to people who win the lottery or who luck into a pile of money. Most of the time, they end up going bankrupt and destroying their lives with bad choices or worse. It sounds crazy, I know, because it is the dream of most everyone. Who would not want a ton of cash without having to do anything for it? Why is it then that hitting the jackpot ends up being catastrophic?

It is the same principle at work. Anything worthwhile must be earned. There are no shortcuts, and the person you become through the striving for something makes you worthy of attaining it. Some of the businessmen and women here in America have made huge fortunes that dwarf those who win lotteries, and it is a rare thing to see them going bankrupt or getting their lives torn apart through their fortunes. You see, Emma, the people they became on the road to achieving their riches made them ready for it. The same is true for me and for you.

I am embarrassed to admit that one of my favorite bands has always been Limp Bizkit. It is super energetic music, and I love the style. I can do without most of the lyrics though. The lead singer has a foul mouth but more importantly, he gets things wrong most of the time. For example, in a song called "Walking Away," he sings, "If I could eliminate all the things that make me frown, take all the baggage that follows me around and just disintegrate it and burn it to the ground." On the surface, who wouldn't want that? It sounds like easy street—no troubles and nothing to make you unhappy.

In fact, it would be a tragedy. Without those painful stepping stones, life would be wasted, and you would never reach the things that you were capable of achieving. The person you were meant to become would never be realized.

So when the going gets tough, obstacles seem to be there at every turn, and the deck seems stacked against you, smile and lean into it. Know that the temporary pain will bring you closer to being the person God meant for you to be.

Love you so much!
Dad

The Fifty-Fifth Letter

Thinking Big

Dear Emma,

Recently, I have been thinking about the things that are accepted as normal in our society. Human beings are social animals, and we live among each other holding onto certain expectations. For example, people expect those around them to act a certain way, behave in a fashion deemed acceptable, and respond to things in a manner that falls within boundaries that are considered "normal."

When things fall outside of these boundaries, we tend to get uncomfortable. Obvious examples on the negative side include the occasional deranged homeless person accosting us in the city, or the loud and sometimes violent confrontations that occur on the trains. We tend to retract quickly, become defensive, and look for the fastest route back to a state of normalcy.

What I have found interesting is that we can get equally uncomfortable when things fall outside of what is considered acceptable and normal on the *positive* side of the ledger. In other words, when a classmate suddenly excels and becomes regionally or nationally recognized. Or when a business colleague hits a jackpot deal or lands a multi-million-dollar client. Someone you know wins the lottery or starts a business that makes it big. There are countless examples on both the negative and positive sides of the spectrum.

The point I am making is simply that as humans, we don't like things that fall outside of our expectations. We go through our days with this craving for security and safety that we feed and protect by looking for normalcy. We want to understand everything and make sure that events, people, and ideas fall into categories that are in the middle of the road.

Here's the problem though: this type of thinking is tragic. It is wrecking our futures and destroying endless possibilities that could easily be ours. Emma, you and I talk all the time about visualizing goals and how important it is to work hard and stay focused on where you want to go. These are the essential elements and disciplines of achievers. The problem is that we are limiting ourselves with little dreams, small goals, and routine visions because we crave "normal." We so desire to maintain our position in the middle of the road that even dreams we consider to be big are really ho-hum.

I've been reading a bit about this business guy named Peter Thiel. The man has made *billions* of dollars and has founded and sold a number of companies including PayPal. Thiel says this, "If you have a 10 year plan, you should ask: Why can't you do this in six months?" His point is simple, we have to throw off our limiting beliefs and pay no attention to what everyone else considers normal.

You see, Emma, the truth is that we have this incredible, God-given power to create our own reality. There are no constraints, limits, or rules other than the ones we place on ourselves or accept from others. To be honest, I am wondering if our dreams and goals are just too small.

Since this is January of a New Year, why don't you and I talk about what we would want to do and become if there were no limits and if nothing was impossible. After that we can plan a way to make it happen!

Love you little one!
Dad

The Fifty-Sixth Letter

Great Expectations

Dear Emma,

For the past few months, I have been thinking about how I can get better at what I do at work. Our team at UBS tries very hard to serve our clients, and we desire strongly to provide them with a fantastic experience. I am always looking to see if we can surpass their anticipations. When they call, I envision them hanging up the phone after speaking with us and feeling grateful that they have us as partners. When we have meetings, I want them to be blown away with our level of concern, knowledge, and thoughtful approaches to help them with their unique challenges.

As Darren Hardy says, "I want to find the line of expectation and then exceed it." Just this past week, I have been seeing if I can work this type of thinking into a larger portion of my life. Work is important—yes, but to be honest, it is only a small component of life. There is so much more. We have relationships, school, friendships, family, sports, recreation, and so many other areas on which to focus.

Every time we do anything, there is a set of expectations that go along with it. For example, your friends expect that you will act a certain way or respond in a typical manner, your teachers anticipate how you will show up in class, your coaches and opponents expect you to perform at a particular level or put out effort at a rate that they have seen before. We also have expectations of ourselves: how hard we will work, what we typically will put up with, and how much we will tolerate. In other words, Emma, we get into a rut. We basically meet people's (and our own) expectations and think that we are doing just fine. I have come to realize that this is a boring way to go through life. If we only meet expectations, we pretty much guarantee that we will be average, mediocre people.

What would happen if we worked to *exceed* expectations in every single thing that we touched? What if we did ten or eleven reps when only eight were called for? What if we stretched ourselves beyond our normal limits in everything we did? For me, that means making a few more calls at work, going the extra mile for my clients, and making sure that I over deliver in every single circumstance.

For you honey, it means studying more than what is required, running an extra set of stairs when training, doing a few more "ghosts" on the squash court, and being more present and more friendly with your peers.

Imagine the results over time!

It's hard not to believe that this is exactly the way God wants us to act. Jesus was always exceeding expectations. Remember when he turned the water into wine? It wasn't just any wine, the steward was so blown away that he went over to the groom at the wedding and pronounced it some of the finest wine ever.

How about when Jesus fed the five thousand people? He started with a few loaves of bread and some fish, and after everyone had eaten their fill, his disciples picked up more than twelve huge baskets of leftovers. The stories are many and the theme is the same: Jesus was always exceeding expectations and going beyond what anyone was anticipating.

Let's you and I make a pact to do the same in everything we do. In school, work, fitness, squash, training, family, friendships—everything! Let's always "find the line of expectation and then exceed it."

Love you honey!
Dad

The
Fifty-Seventh Letter

Don't Play it Safe

Dear Emma,

The dangers of life are infinite and among them is safety.

I stumbled across this recently and fell in love with it. A German philosopher and playwright named Johann von Goethe wrote it way back in the 1800s. The phrase may seem to make no sense at all when you first read it, after all—what could possibly be dangerous about safety?

We often forget that this life we live is incredibly short. We have so little time on this earth, and there is so much to see, do, be, and have. Von Goethe was suggesting that we risk missing out on the greatest of all adventures by constantly seeking safety, security, and comfort. Those things may feel good in the moment, but if we always look for them, we will end up with tons of regrets and unaccomplished dreams.

The Rocking Chair test is something that I have made up for myself years ago. I frequently envision your mom and me at the end of our lives sitting on a beautiful porch in two white high-backed rocking chairs. The sun is setting over meadows and fields as we sit holding hands watching the evening arrive. Our faces are deeply lined bearing faint smiles of gratitude and contentment. You see, Emma, the one thing that I know that would disturb this scene would be a heart full of regrets.

When I make decisions, even small ones, I want them to pass the Rocking Chair test. For me, that means making sure that what I am seeking to do (or not do) won't disturb that vision of your mom and me. It's interesting too, more often than not, that means doing things that make me step out of my comfort zone. It means taking risks, putting myself out there, and doing things that make me uncomfortable. In other words, it means *not* playing it safe.

Don't misunderstand me, I am not suggesting that we all become daredevils, undertake foolish stunts, or even act carelessly. I simply think that we should always look for ways to stretch ourselves. We should push to grow, to try, to do things that require a little bit of courage.

Here's a great example: over dinner recently, we talked about always being first. Meaning, being the first one to smile at a stranger, the first one to say hello, the first one to introduce ourselves and strike up a conversation. Doing so might make you feel uncool or nervous but who cares! It is such an easy thing and makes a huge difference amidst a sea of lonely and insecure people.

This world is huge and the possibilities for you are endless. Our family talks often about how you can do anything that you want if you set your mind to it. Think of your grandfather with his incredible artistic talent. Many of the beautiful paintings in our home are the work of his hands. In every single circumstance, he started with a blank canvas—just a piece of cloth. In the same way, Emma, you are standing in front of a blank canvas, and it is up to you to envision, design, and paint your life's journey. Don't play it safe, honey. Make your painting colorful, beautiful, and vibrant—rich with relationships, travels, and adventures.

I can't wait to see how it turns out!

All my love,
Dad

The
Fifty-Eighth Letter

F6

Dear Emma,

I would never get a tattoo; it's just not my thing. I would be nervous about permanently marking my skin with something that would likely cause me serious regret down the road.

Still... What if? What if I was interested in getting a tattoo? What would it be? What possibly could be so monumental, so important, and so compelling as to warrant its existence on my skin permanently for me and the entire world to see? To a certain extent, a tattoo defines a person. People will immediately draw conclusions and cast judgments (rightly or wrongly) about the wearer. Like it or not, that's how it works.

One of my favorite authors Ryan Holiday has two tattoos. On one forearm, he has written in block letters, "The Obstacle is the Way," in order to remind himself that it is challenges and adversities that move us forward and enable us to get better. On the other forearm is written, "Ego is the Enemy," a statement that spells out the dangers of conceit and an inflated opinion of oneself. I totally get it, and I like it.

So Emma, your Dad's tattoo would be simple. It would read "F6," and it would be a reminder to me of the six most important things in my life. The things that define me, consume me, and give me purpose. They are the things I constantly think about, pray about, and shape my existence around.

Faith is the first. You know how important my relationship with God is to me. I am so grateful for his gifts and his engagement in our lives. I can feel his love, support, and encouragement every day. It is like a warm hand on my shoulder. Sometimes I feel that if I turn my head and look behind me, I would see him standing right there. Every morning, I start my day with prayer and meditation, and the power I derive from it is impossible to describe.

Second is family. Oh my are we blessed… Your mother, you, your brother, and sister are absolutely everything to me. The things I do are all for you. I was put on this earth to pour my heart and soul into you, and my greatest joy is to serve you with everything that I am or will ever be.

Fitness is the third "F." Our bodies are gifts from God, and I believe he would want us to keep them in amazing condition. I have found also that being fit has huge rewards in terms of energy, positive mindset, health, and attitude.

Fortitude is fourth. Of all the values and character traits that I admire, fortitude is the one that I strive for and cherish the most. It is grit, determination, and strength under pressure. A person who has fortitude never quits no matter how many times they are knocked down. Adversity does nothing but sharpen their character. I want to be a man of fortitude.

Finances are fifth on my list. Although money has nothing to do with happiness, a certain amount of it affords our family choices, security, and safety. I am committed to being a provider for you and our family, and I am focused on ensuring that our finances are solid.

Finally, there is fun! I am convinced that God wants us to enjoy his amazing creation. We only get one life to live, and we need to enjoy it. The laughter we share and the fun we have together are the things that can never be taken away even if our circumstances crumble. Let's seek the goodness in all things and never take ourselves too seriously.

So there you have it, Emma. "F6" would be my tattoo. What would yours be?

Love you so much!
Dad

The
Fifty-Ninth Letter

The Waiting

Dear Emma,

Tom Petty is a legendary classic rock musician who is still active after something like forty years of touring and making records. I never really cared for his music, but after all those years, his songs have been played with such regularity that a few of the lyrics stick in your head.

One of his most famous pieces of music is called "The Waiting." It was produced back in 1981, and like the rest of his stuff, it's just not my style. What I remember (and think about often) though is the opening line of the song. It says simply, "The waiting is the hardest part." And that, Emma, is one hundred percent true.

We just came back from yet another squash tournament, and once again, you came so close... It was devastating for me to watch you lose in the quarterfinals in a brutal five game match after being up 2–0. I was brokenhearted for you, honey, and I had to leave the building afterward to get a hold of myself. Truth be told, I was mad at God and angry at the universe over it. I know how hard you work. I see the sacrifices you make. I can feel the callouses on your right hand when I hold it. As your father, I was desperate to see you paid back for the years of punishing training and the oceans of blood, sweat, and tears.

I went outside and could barely raise my head. I called your mom back in Chicago, and we talked through it. She brought me some peace (as she usually does), but it was the still small voice that quieted my spirit that day. That voice simply said, "Wait."

I had an assurance right then that your day will most certainly come. I could envision you holding that winner's trophy and the tears coming again, only this time, they would be tears of joy and triumph.

You see, Emma, God's timing is always perfect while ours is not. He knows the best moment for us to plant the flag on the mountaintop. While Tom Petty had it right when he said that the waiting is the hardest part, he probably didn't think about the rewards that come from waiting. This is the time that God uses to form our character, to make us tougher, to keep us humble, and to remind us that we are not in control.

Remember King David from the Bible? He was just a shepherd boy in the fields when he was anointed to be the next king of Israel. Do you know what happened next? The answer is virtually nothing. He spent the next thirteen years waiting for his destiny to unfold. Truthfully, much of those years were incredibly brutal as the reigning King Saul chased him endlessly seeking to take his life.

The lesson from David comes from how he acted during those thirteen long years. Most people would have gotten bitter and resentful. They would have quit trying and given up on all their dreams. Not David. He spent those thirteen years believing that his time would come. He committed to getting better every day, he trained patiently, and he waited—knowing that his vision would become a reality. His belief never wavered.

Wait for it, Emma. Be like David. Believe. Train. Dream. Your time is coming just as surely as the sun rises in the morning.

Love you oh so much!
Dad

The Sixtieth Letter

Lessons from Losing

Dear Emma,

I continue to be fascinated with the ancient Stoic philosophers. It's amazing to read their words from thousands of years ago and feel the similarity in their lives and struggles. Their world was essentially the same as ours with the exception of technology.

Remember when we went through the ruins of Pompeii—the city in Italy caught by surprise by an erupting volcano? We toured the streets together and were fascinated to see where the ancient people had gone for their fast-food, their dry-cleaning, and their groceries. Their houses were the same, their parks, and squares similar to ours.

No surprise then to understand that their lives were the same as well.

I am thinking about this now because I just returned from a business trip to Park City, Utah with my business teammate, Jake Graves. Jake was a college ski racer at the University of New Hampshire and grew up racing in the western mountains. His journey was similar to yours in the athletic context. Sponsorships, travel, endless practice, and sacrifice were part of his skiing life just like they are part of your squash life.

Over coffee one morning, I asked him about his experience in youth ski racing. His immediate response startled me with its honesty. "It sucked," Jake said, "You are constantly losing." He paused for a moment and then continued reflectively, "I learned a ton, though."

Sounds familiar, I bet! By the way, there is absolutely nothing wrong with losing if you: (1) Learn from it and (2) Always hate it. Those two ingredients make losing actually one of the most beneficial things that can happen to you.

Look what I found from the philosopher Seneca written to one of his students Lucilius more than two thousand years ago:

> No prize fighter can go with high spirits into the strife if he has never been beaten black and blue; the only contestant who can confidently enter the lists is the man who has seen his own blood, who has felt his teeth rattle beneath his opponent's fist, who has been tripped and felt the full force of his adversary's charge, who has been downed in body but not in spirit, one who, as often as he falls, rises again with greater defiance than ever.

Seneca had it exactly right all those years ago. None of us can get better unless we lose. Not just lose either but lose badly. Have our teeth rattled and get really beat-up.

Every time it happens, it has to hurt, and we have to learn from it. We have to get up every single time and let the fever of defiance burn inside more brightly than ever. That's the recipe for greatness and the path towards becoming who you want to become.

So you see, Emma, the road you travel today is much like the road traveled by people striving to achieve their dreams throughout human history. Just stay after it!

Love you so much,
Dad

The Sixty-First Letter

More on Love

Dear Emma,

I often write to you about experiences, things that I have been reading, or thoughts on the challenges you face as you pass through your teenage years. We also talk constantly of our goals, dreams, and the plans we have for achieving them. Those things find their way into these letters frequently as well. The shared journey we have with our athletic pursuits is binding for us and gives us endless topics for conversation.

My letter to you now has nothing to do with any of those things. In fact, dearest Emma, this is perhaps the most important thing that I have ever written to you. I want you to hear me clearly, stop what you are doing, and focus absolutely on what you will be reading. Let it seep into your spirit and fill you.

The short version is simply this: You are loved. Absolutely. Unconditionally. Massively.

I vividly remember the day you were born and can still picture the nurse handing you to your mother in your swaddling blankets. Tears of love poured from both of us as we covered you in kisses and held your tiny hands.

That same love continues. It burns inside of us and exists with the same intensity as it did on the very first day of your life. It is there despite the distractions, emotions, challenges, and uncertainties that surround us. Your performance has no bearing on it, your perceived failures and successes do not impact it. It is not earned nor does it increase or decrease by virtue of your actions or your words. It cannot be broken, changed, or impacted. It is absolutely permanent and immovable.

As big as our love is for you, honey, it is nothing compared to God's love for all of us. He holds us in the palm of his hand and protects us in the shadow of his wings. There is nothing we can do to escape his love or cause him to turn away his shining face from us. We clearly don't deserve it, but yet there it is—inexplicable and incredible. A force that is stronger than any other. I can feel it sometimes in random moments usually in the still in-betweens. When action ebbs, and I feel grateful for the smallest things. When my breath slows, and my mind unclutters.

Those moments make life worth living even more so than the mountaintop celebrations of goals achieved and obstacles conquered.

My wish for you, Emma, is simply that you feel this love—the love that radiates from God and from your mother and me. I pray that is surrounds you, envelops you, and gives you a peace and confidence that nothing on this earth can shake.

Know now and always how deeply you are loved.

XO,
Dad

The Sixty-Second Letter

New Thought

Dear Emma,

I've long admired many of the views held by those who espouse the New Thought movement. This system of beliefs was formulated in the nineteenth century and is still quite strong today. Visualization, personal power, positive thinking, and the law of attraction all emanate from New Thought. The older I get, the more I am convicted about them—quite simply because they have been proven absolutely true in my own life and in the lives of others who think along these lines.

Honey, we have talked quite a bit about the immense power of self-belief, self-confidence, and seeing yourself as being the person you aspire to be. I want you to understand that this process is not just one way to succeed in the achievement of your goals but rather the *only* way. You see, dear, life unfolds from your own beliefs. If you have an unshakeable view of yourself as who you want to become, it will invariably and without a doubt come to be true in real life. Don't be misled—it is not at all easy. The mental work around this is incredibly hard and takes real effort. You have to focus daily on it, endlessly will yourself forward, develop statements on which you ceaselessly meditate, and have a firm belief that what you desire will come into being.

All this may sound a bit "out there", but did you know that the concept was espoused by Jesus? Throughout the gospels, Jesus works miracles simply by believing that what he wills to happen will invariably happen. In Mark 11, he shares the secret to all that will listen: "Whatever you ask for when you pray, believe that you have received it and it will be yours." Notice the verb tense—Jesus is telling us to believe that we have something before it is ours yet.

Remember, life unfolds from the inside out. If you believe that you have something or are someone intensely enough—it will invariably happen in your life. Such is the promise of God. Doubting it would be a direct contradiction of Christ's words.

Recently, I shared with you a few paragraphs that I wrote for myself years ago. I recite these words many times a day and believe them as firmly as I believe the sun will rise in the morning. When I wrote them years ago, it was an uncertain time in my career, and the weight of providing for you and the family was really heavy on me. Those words were a statement of my future state, a promise of the things that would be mine. I made myself believe that they were absolutely true—even if an outsider might have disagreed with me or even scoffed at me. Guess what? Most of them are true now, and the rest are coming into being.

For you, write down what you want and describe in detail who you want to become. Internalize it, believe it, and go through your days acting like those things are already yours. The college you want to attend, the goals you set with your squash coach, the grades you want to see on your report card, the scores you want on your standardized tests should all be carefully laid out. Believe these things will come to pass with intensity and conviction and without a doubt, they will.

Love you!
Dad

The
Sixty-Third Letter

Prophesy your Future

Dear Emma,

When someone asks you how you are doing—what is your answer?

Today, I noticed just how many people gave me mumbled responses, complaints, or faint-hearted "okays" when I greeted them. How sad! These are good people, and little do they know that they are setting themselves up for failure in multiple ways. First, nobody wants to hang around with negative, low-energy people. They might as well pin a sign on their chest warning away potential friends, new associations, or even soul mates. Secondly, last month I wrote a letter about how life unfolds from within. If you believe that the concept is true, then you can clearly see why it's a bit dangerous to tell people that you are doing just fine when they ask or worse yet relate to them your troubles. Doing so will invite negativity and bad vibes into your life as surely as the sun rises in the morning.

When someone asks how you are, tell them you are doing incredibly well. Tell them things are great and that you are having a fantastic day. Radiate enthusiasm, positive energy, and a grateful spirit. People will be drawn to you like magnets if you do this, and you will find that your own mood and day will brighten also.

Emma, the things you believe to be true in your life will come to pass even if you can't feel them in the moment. What makes this process infinitely more powerful and rapid is when you give voice to your beliefs. Quite simply, you speak them into existence.

History abounds with stories of people who have proclaimed the seemingly impossible. Henry Ford, Abraham Lincoln, Michael Jordan, and countless others have made proclamations that caused others to scoff and make fun of them. It didn't matter to them—they were prophesying their futures.

Joseph, one of the great heroes of the Old Testament, believed so strongly in his future success that he told his brothers that he would be the greatest of them all. They became so angry with him that they sold him off as a slave. Despite that setback (and many others), Joseph went on to fulfill his vision and became the most powerful man in Egypt.

For you and I, the lesson is to speak our future. We need to give it voice, and we need to proclaim it into reality. It might feel a bit silly at first—it certainly did for me. I can tell you though, Emma, the embarrassment quickly fades when your dreams and goals start becoming reality. In the morning and all through the day, I speak my purpose, my goals, and my beliefs. As I walk through the city, you will sometimes see my lips moving as I softly prophesy what I know will be coming true in my life. Does that sounds strange? Maybe! But man, oh, man does it work!

How badly do you want the goals that you have laid out for yourself? Who are you in two years and in five years? Where are you? What are you doing? Script out that perfect vision of yourself and burn it into your mind's eye. Believe it to be true and be absolutely convinced that it will come to pass. Thank God that it is already a reality in your life and then give voice to it. Speak it with an unshakeable faith all day and every day.

I can see us now—smiling and laughing—the day you tell me that your dreams came true. Just like you scripted them!

Love you so much (proud of you too)!
Dad

The
Sixty-Forth Letter

Comparison

Dear Emma,

I can't remember a time in my life when I was not competitive with those around me. I always wanted to be the best at what I was doing, and I still crave respect, admiration, and accolades. For all this time, I have fervently believed that competition was the key contributor of success and the ingredient that drove all achievers to new heights. The huge problem though with endless and runaway competition with others is that it breeds discontent, frustration, and even self-hatred. It's a dangerous path, honey, and one that I want you to really think about in your own life. You see, the problem with endless competition with others is that you are always comparing yourself to them.

Teddy Roosevelt, the twenty-sixth president of the United States said wisely, "Comparison is the thief of joy." The people around you in school, on the train, on the squash court, and in all your peer groups are not running your race. They are running their own. God created all of us uniquely and in his image and likeness. We are his individual masterpieces and infused with distinct talents, dreams, and preferences. I firmly believe as I write this that He would probably be a bit confused as to why we would go about comparing ourselves to one another.

You probably have found out as I have that trying *not* to compare ourselves to others is one of life's great challenges. Our western society is built around comparison. It is central to product and lifestyle marketing, fashion, performance measurement, benchmarking, and even class ranking at your school. The pressure to perform is tough enough without the weight of hearing about or watching firsthand someone do something better/faster than you. For me, it usually comes up around wealth, business achievement, or possessions. It has been all too easy in my life to get into the trap of comparing myself to others who have more. Wow, is it painful when I get in that mode! I can easily get hot with envy, ridden with anxiety, and beat myself up terribly for not being "good enough."

Emma, I think you and I are a lot alike, and I desperately don't want you to go through the pain and suffering that I have in this area. Let's work on this together.

Here's a few thoughts that are helping me:

- We are enough as we are. God loves us incredibly because we are His and not because of where we stand versus others.
- He has given us unique abilities, and I believe he would like to see us simply develop those to the extent we can. Remember always that He does not put a dream in our hearts without granting us the capacity to achieve it.
- The word "competition" comes from a Latin root meaning "conspire together." We are not called to beat out people in this life, but rather we have an opportunity to make each other better. "As iron sharpens iron, so one man sharpens another," says Proverbs 27.
- In a sense, we are all one. We are created as God's own children and called above all else to love God and one another. When we truly embrace this love and let it seep into our spirit, I find that it leaves precious little room for any of the destructive thoughts associated with the curse of comparison.

From now forward, honey, when you step onto the squash court facing a tough opponent, think about how the coming match will give you both an opportunity to learn and get better. Conspire together to improve. When your thoughts take you down a path toward "not good enough" or "can't measure up to," just feel God's delight in you and bask in his unconditional love. Remember always too that Mom and I love you so much, and our love has nothing to do with how you look, rank, dress, or perform. You are magnificent just as you are.

Xoxoxo.
Dad

The Sixty-Fifth Letter

Mindset

Dear Emma,

I am so glad that you recommended Carol Dweck's awesome book, *Mindset*. It's not that many of the concepts are new to us—we talk often about the importance of being goal driven and the power of self-belief. The impact of the book for me is more about identifying the state of my own thinking in any given moment and then teaching myself to shift, to learn, and then to grow.

You remember that Dweck identifies and discusses two mental mindsets: the growth mind-set and the fixed mind-set. Though there are many nuances to her definitions, in essence, she reveals that growth-minded people are hungry to learn and develop. They believe that there is no limit to their abilities if they continue to push forward and challenge themselves. There is no real failure in their lives but rather only opportunities to learn. Fixed-minded people want desperately to be recognized as intelligent or talented but will only participate in things that will solidify their position. The fear of failure or the perception that they will lose respect and self-esteem in new ventures kills their appetite to accept challenges. They hate feeling vulnerable and have a strong desire to be highly valued. Anything that might threaten the way they are perceived in the world is to be avoided.

Despite all my talk and work over the years around personal development, I still feel much of Dweck's fixed mind-set traits alive within me. I also recognize that there is huge power in exposing them and knowing that I can change the mind-set. Will you work on this with me? Here are some of the areas I am thinking about:

1. It's important to me to feel respected. While there is nothing wrong with this (I suspect most people want the same thing), it is holding me back from learning new things and trying different angles. I am unwilling to "embrace the suck" as the military expression goes. I don't want to risk my fragile ego by starting from scratch. Push me on this.

2. I have a tough time viewing a failure as anything but a failure. In my business, if I have a deal go south or lose a client, I feel terrible about it, and my mind races all the way into self-doubt and dire consequences. I loved the way that Dweck described the growth-minded children she was working with on page 4, "Not only weren't they not discouraged by failure, they didn't even think they were failing. They thought they were learning." I see huge opportunities with this way of thinking and a lot less stress as well.

3. Believe it or not, I have held a rather limited view of my own intelligence. Dweck points out that IQ is not a fixed measurement and that intelligence is something that can be expanded through work, study, and self-challenge. The thought is exciting and opens up new horizons for me. It also gives me more confidence and allows me to be more open and curious with people who may know more about a topic (at the time) then I do. Before, I would have been fearful to ask "dumb" questions. I believe now that I have the capacity to learn about anything. Intelligence is merely about plugging knowledge gaps.

There is tons more in this book that we should chat about, honey, as it is so relevant to our lives. How can I help you around the concepts that Dweck lays out? What are the applications from the book that you are working on? How are you applying the principles to your squash career? Your high-school life?

Can't wait to process it together a bit more. I guess that's all for now, rock star. Here's wishing for constant growth and learning for both of us!

Love you!
Dad

The Sixty-Sixth Letter

Peaks and Valleys

Dear Emma,

So much has happened since my last letter to you. The ebbs and flows of life are constant and it is so important to remember that we cannot let ourselves be governed by current circumstances. So many people go through life allowing their happiness to be dictated by what is happening in the moment. If something breaks their way, they feel good and if they get twisted up somehow, their world falls apart.

I've been thinking of the peaks and valleys in your life over the last month, honey. You just got back from Canada where you played for the USA National Squash Team in our nation's matches versus Canada. Not only did you get to represent our country but you won your match securing an overall victory for the United States! What a mountaintop experience!

On the other hand, there have been challenges.. Despite your hard work in preparing for the ACT test, your second practice exam came back with a score that was far lower than you had expected and below your original score. Ouch!

You can see in your own life how easy it is to let circumstances and events dictate your happiness and also how you feel about your self. In a way, we are all like ping pong balls, if we let ourselves, we just get batted around from one extreme emotion to another. Joy and euphoria to sadness and pain in the blink of an eye.

To be honest, I totally struggle with this. You know that I work in the Wealth Management business handling clients' money. Our team has them invested in the capital markets and if I let myself, I find it easy to be ecstatic when the markets are rising and depressed when they are falling. Like that ping pong ball, I can easily let myself get knocked all over the place.

We've got to guard against this type of thing and I have a few thoughts on how to do it.

First off, we need to ground ourselves in gratitude. We've talked about this before and I don't think it can be overemphasized. When we feel like we are suffocating or that "bad" things are happening, it's hugely helpful to simply breathe and think about the amazing blessings in or life. An intense focus on God's goodness, His gifts to us, the air, sky, wind on our faces and the beauty that surrounds us can transport us away from the emotion of the moment and bring around a peace and steadfastness.

Another thing that is massively helpful is to simply ignore the noise. I know you love social media, Ems, and feel it is the way that your generation maintains friendships and engages with one another. That is probably true and I am just wondering if perhaps placing some boundaries on it might be a good thing to try. When we let ourselves be constantly barraged by media of any type; social, news, print, TV—anything—we allow others to get into our heads, distract us and in some ways tell us how we should be feeling. All kinds of negative stuff can come from too much media exposure; jealousy, envy, frustration, anger, sadness, you name it. Let's not let anyone else dictate the course of our day or shape how it is that we are feeling.

Finally, honey, know this—you and I can be who we will to be. The knowledge and power that resides in that fundamental truth is awesome beyond description and can easily carry us through any stormy weather, temporary setback or tough situation. Keep your eye on your goal and it will be yours.

Love you so much!
Dad

The Sixty-
Seventh Letter

Noise

Dear Emma,

I've pretty much stopped reading or watching any type of news media. My work at UBS requires me to be up to speed on the financial happenings but the rest of it is not helpful at all to me. News channels and outlets are money makers and they are in the business of getting us all to watch, read and focus on their products. The easiest way for them to do so is to relentlessly seek and disseminate all the negative things in our world. Whether it's a plane crash, a natural disaster, a politician saying something ridiculous or a celebrity getting divorced—most people eat it up. It's entertainment to them, a way of taking the focus off of themselves. The reality is that an obsession with it can kill their chances to reach their goals.

Don't get me wrong, honey, there is nothing wrong with keeping current with what is happening in the world. But you and I know that what we focus on in our lives inevitably expands. We become what we think about. If we allow a daily barrage of negativity into our lives, it will distract us from the things that we want to bring to us.

It's not just the news either. I believe that we should all be hyper vigilant on who we hang out with, what we listen to, what we watch and what stories we tell ourselves. We need to surround ourselves with positive energy by making sure that the things we let into our lives are encouraging us, uplifting us and helping us get to where we want to go.

I recently went through my cell phone contact list and deleted everyone that I felt wasn't a positive influence in my life. It wasn't easy. Some of these people I have known for a long time. I must admit also that it took a while—there were an awful lot of people that when I really thought about it—were holding me back in some way. It's not that they meant to, it's just that their view of the world might have been a bit negative or they didn't share my belief that there are no limits to what we can be or what we can do.

I know I am talking now mostly about cutting things out of our lives but the opposite is hugely important also. We must also be adding things in that will help us get to where we want to go. People that are aiming high in their own lives and are encouraging us to push higher. Music with lyrics that showcase big goals and big beliefs. Podcasts that uplift and share the stories of people who have accomplished their dreams. Books that inspire and instruct.

The final piece is what Charles Haanel calls, "The Silence", in his great book, *The Master Key System*. He is talking about meditation. You don't have to overthink this. For us as Christians, much of it is simply a prayerful focus on what you are seeking. Remember what Jesus said, "Whatever you ask for when you pray, believe that you have received it and it will be yours." You know that I meditate every day and combine it with prayer, bible reading and a deep focus on the things that I am working towards. One of our family's favorite expressions is "All things"—as in all things always come to me. The funny thing is that they inevitably do. Always.

Follow what I have laid out here and the same will happen for you. Always!

Love you!
Dad

The Sixty-Eighth Letter

Archilochus

Dear Emma,

You and I are much alike. We have big goals that we obsess about and dreams that we desperately want to come true in our lives. We work, strive, reach and push -sacrificing much on the road to achieve the visions before us.

I have been rereading some of the stoic philosophers from ancient Greece and the following caught my eye from Archilochus, "We don't rise to the level of our expectation, we fall to the level of our training."

Think about that for a minute. It was eye opening for me.

You see, Emma, everyone wants to be successful. Everyone has dreams that they want to come true in their lives. We have talked often about how important it is to visualize ourselves as having already achieved the things that we have been working for. While it is true that we must believe in ourselves first and foremost, the second part of the equation is work. Most people fall down on this one. By the way, too, it's not just putting in the time—it's training with a laser-like focus and intensity.

Remember our trip to Philadelphia for your squash tournament? We had a chance to watch a few of the professional squash players train before their matches at The US Open. Wow. It was next level stuff. Intention. Focus. Intensity. They weren't just going through the motions or checking the box. They were dialed in and getting after it.

It was a reminder to me that if we want to get to the top of a mountain, we have to want it. Want it badly enough to work like no one else will. Those squash pros have incredible athletic gifts, great hand eye coordination and access to world class coaching. But the truth is—so do thousands of others. The difference maker is not their raw talent—it's their desire coupled with their focus.

I saw a t-shirt the other day that said—DEF. Below the letters was written, "Discipline Equals Freedom". I recognized the slogan as coming from a podcast personality, Jocko Willink, one of the most famous veterans from the Navy Seal Teams. Daily discipline does equal freedom. Making the hard choices in terms of diet, work, fitness and study will set you up for massive success and take you well above everyone else.

You have chosen a difficult path, honey, with your athletic pursuits. Your dedication thus far has placed you as one of the top ten squash players in the nation for your age group. As Jessie Itzler says though, "you didn't come this far just to come this far".

As colleges now circle around you, you have an opportunity to separate yourself even further. You can reach higher levels—if that is your choice—and become even better at the game you love. The first key lies in the statement from Archilochus about the intensity and level of our training.

In closing, dear one, know always that I am here for you. I will be your biggest fan and your most loyal supporter. I will suffer with you, cry with you and finally celebrate with you on your mountaintop.

Love you!
Dad

The Sixty-Ninth Letter

Blake

Dear Emma,

Sometimes I feel like I have been completely on the wrong path. Fooled by the giant machinery of our society. Sucked along with the masses that believe blindly that more is better. Pulled into the current of accumulation and into the false assumption that my happiness, personal value or satisfaction with life will be enhanced by the acquisition of yet another thing.

The trap is there in plain sight for all to see yet we fall into it so easily. Slick advertisements showcasing the shiny and new, pressures from friends to keep up, the perceived judgment of others who try and make us feel unworthy or less than.

The false assumption that security and joy come from possessions is a dangerous path as it leads only to an endless treadmill of wanting. For you and me also, the drive to compete can fuel our speed down this dark road as we constantly want to out do other people or somehow prove ourselves to be better than. Our competitive nature is a gift from God but it can easily be used against us in this arena.

What's especially terrifying is that few people ever learn. We crave and strive for something, giddily acquire it and then a short time later realize that our happiness is unchanged. The emptiness felt before is still present and if anything, the weight of our possessions adds complexity and needless cares into our lives. We then compound the sadness with regret. And then we do it all over again. Endlessly working towards filling the void.

I don't want this for you, honey.

Jesus tells a story in Luke, Chapter 12, about a rich man who had accumulated so much that he decided to tear down his old storehouses and build new ones just to hold it all. But God said to him, "You fool! This very night your life will be required of you. Then who will own what you have accumulated?" Don't misunderstand me, Ems, there is nothing wrong at all with prosperity. In fact, God wants it for us. The bible is full of the promises of God and his desire for abundance for us. We just run into trouble quickly if we let the pursuit of things and "more" become all consuming.

Recently, I had the opportunity to head off to the Georgia Mountains to attend a camp put on by Jessie Itzler. It was awesome and I know I have been gushing on and on about it. I don't think I told you though about the new friends I made in Chadd and Blake Wright. These two brothers live down in the mountains of Georgia and are two of the most grounded, happiest and faith-filled people I have come across in a very long time. I've been chatting with Blake a bit recently and have enjoyed our growing relationship so much.

Our backgrounds are so different, our lifestyles dissimilar in every way yet I feel myself drawn to him. It's his honesty and innate goodness that attracted me first but as I thought more deeply on it, I recognized that he has a certain detachment about him. An unspoken indifference to the things of this world and instead a keen and Godly interest in people, experiences and his surroundings. I imagine he would be an endless frustration to all advertisers and marketers—a stone wall in their efforts to convince him that he is not enough or somehow in need of the latest "thing".

Let's try together to be more like Blake. More present, more detached, more focused on others. I think it would lead to a deeper peace for both of us.

Love you so much,
Dad

The Seventieth Letter

The Raven

Dear Emma,

Every single day for the last forty years, Robert "Raven" Kraft has run eight miles on Miami Beach. Every Day. No breaks, no misses and no excuses.

The accomplishment is staggering and it's no surprise that Raven is known now throughout the world. A few weeks ago, I went down and joined what has become known as "The Raven Run". In the last twenty-one years, Kraft has only run alone three times—and those times fell in the midst of hurricanes. People come from all over the planet to run with him, spend time with him and see if they can gain an understanding of what makes him tick.

Our group was a typical mix of people from all over—there were several Canadians, a state trooper from New Jersey and a smattering of locals to round things out. None of us knew what to expect as we started out but we all recognized that we were in the presence of someone very special. What kind of man has the sheer force of will to run eight miles every day for forty years? How does so much discipline and determination get packed into one person?

Kraft's body is not what it used to be and he suffers from terrible back pain. He is bent over at the waist a bit yet is lean, strong and bronzed from the Florida sun. As we set off together at a slow trot, this man's incredible story unfolded. It all started forty years ago at a rough point in Kraft's life. He sought an outlet in running and had no intention of doing it every day—it just happened. He felt better both physically and mentally from the exercise and the days on the beach turned into weeks then into months and then into years.

There is learning in all things and as our group trotted along and talked, we were rewarded with a good bit of it. Here are a few things that I have been thinking about:

- Consistency may be one of the most powerful forces in nature. This man didn't really do anything spectacular—he just repeated the same thing relentlessly and the result is worldwide fame. I am wondering in my own life where I can apply this same unceasing type of effort. The image in my mind is of the way a steady stream of water can cut through rock given time and consistency.

- Kraft also loves people and is truly interested in them. On our run, he sought to really get to know each one of us. He listened, probed—he looked for intimacy and relationship. I have to recognize that I can't hit my goals and ambitions by myself—I need help, I need good people in my life who are building me up and running the race with me. And yes, I need to do the same for others.

- Sometimes, we all have to just keep moving forward—even if it is just a small step at a time. Big goals can be over-whelming with their size, complexity and obstacles. The Raven doesn't think about the enormity of the task of run-ning eight miles every day for the last forty years. He thinks about simply reaching and passing the next lifeguard sta-tion on the beach during the present moment.

- Most people start something with excitement and enthu-siasm. They make commitments, promises to themselves and then before you know it, they quit, get tired or forget about their initial passion. It's amazing how special we can become if we just exercise our God given self-discipline (remember the fruit of the Spirit in Galatians 5:22?). Look at the fame Kraft has.

I am getting down to Miami a few times a year now to see clients and I think I will run with Raven again. Not for the work out but for the continued gift of knowledge. There seems to be a fair bit of wisdom in an old guy on the beach in Miami.

Love you honey!
Dad

About the Author

Allen Carter is first and foremost a loving husband and a devoted father. By day, he leads a team of eight people at one of the world's largest financial services firms. His group is dedicated to serving individuals and families with financial, retirement, and investment planning. Relationships are everything to Allen, and his love of people is reflected in his writing, his work, and his life.

The Carter family calls Chicago home even though Claire lives and works in New York, and Wells is now in Salt Lake. Mary and Allen are fortunate to have their youngest, Emma, still at home and are savoring her high school years before her inevitable flight from the nest.

Allen is active in the community and committed to giving back with his time, talent, and treasure. He serves on the board of trustees of Marillac St. Vincent Family Services, and his previous board positions include The Judd Goldman Adaptive Sailing Foundation, St. Joseph Services, the University Club of Chicago, and others.

Along with a number of professional designations, Allen holds a BA from Hillsdale College with a degree in English and Business. In his spare time, he can be found sailing on Lake Michigan, working out, traveling, and using any excuse possible to get outside to enjoy God's beautiful creation.

Connect with him on LinkedIn and on all the socials— @alleninchicago.